PENGUIN
SPECIALS

T0359387

Penguin Specials fill a gap. Written by some of today's most exciting and insightful writers, they are short enough to be read in a single sitting — when you're stuck on a train; in your lunch hour; between dinner and bedtime. Specials can provide a thought-provoking opinion, a primer to bring you up to date, or a striking piece of fiction. They are concise, original and affordable.

To browse digital and print Penguin Specials titles, please refer to **penguin.com.au/penguinspecials**

LOWY INSTITUTE

The Lowy Institute is an independent, nonpartisan international policy think tank. The Institute provides high-quality research and distinctive perspectives on the issues and trends shaping Australia's role in the world. The Lowy Institute Papers are peer-reviewed essays and research papers on key international issues affecting Australia and the world.

For a discussion on *Morrison's Mission: How a beginner reshaped Australian foreign policy* with Paul Kelly and leading commentators, visit the Lowy Institute's daily commentary and analysis site, *The Interpreter*: **lowy institute.org/the-interpreter/debate/morrisons-mission**.

Paul Kelly is Editor-at-Large for *The Australian*.
He has covered Australian governments from
Gough Whitlam to Scott Morrison. He is the author
of many books including *The End of Certainty* on
the politics and economics of the 1980s, and the
Lowy Institute Paper *Howard's Decade*.

LOWY INSTITUTE

Morrison's Mission

How a beginner reshaped Australian foreign policy

A LOWY INSTITUTE PAPER

PAUL KELLY

PENGUIN BOOKS

UK | USA | Canada | Ireland | Australia
India | New Zealand | South Africa | China

Penguin Books is part of the Penguin Random House group of companies
whose addresses can be found at global.penguinrandomhouse.com.

Penguin
Random House
Australia

First published by Penguin Books, 2022

Cover photograph by Sam Mooy/Stringer via Getty Images
Typeset by Midland Typesetters, Australia

Printed and bound in Australia by Griffin Press, an accredited
ISO AS/NZS 14001 Environmental Management Systems printer

A catalogue record for this
book is available from the
National Library of Australia

ISBN 978 0 14377 804 2

penguin.com.au

CONTENTS

Preface

This Lowy Institute Paper is an account of Scott Morrison as a foreign policy prime minister during a period of unpredictable change. Its primary task is to outline the contours of his policy, examine how it evolved and understand the distinctive features of his thinking and style.

This follows an earlier Lowy Institute Paper I wrote in 2006 on John Howard's foreign policy, titled *Howard's Decade*. While there are parallels between Howard and Morrison, the contrasts are also noteworthy given the different eras in which they governed and the different challenges they have faced.

The deadline for this Paper was extended to allow coverage of the AUKUS agreement between Australia, the United Kingdom and United States. But it could not be stretched to include a full assessment of climate change and the 2021 UN Climate Change Conference in Glasgow. In a rapidly changing world, there is no natural termination point for a project such as this.

In preparing this Paper, I conducted a series of interviews and drew on others that I conducted during the year for my columns in *The Australian*. I conducted a long interview for the Paper with Scott Morrison, followed by further discussions and assistance from his office. I also conducted on-record interviews with Marise Payne, Alex Hawke, Dave Sharma, Mike Burgess, Duncan Lewis, Dennis Richardson, Richard Maude, Allan Gyngell, Peter Varghese, Linda Jakobson, Bruce Miller and Marcus Hellyer.

I drew upon several discussions with Malcolm Turnbull, Josh Frydenberg, Simon Birmingham and Penny Wong that I conducted when writing my weekly columns. In addition, I spoke off-record with many people still in the 'system' and involved with Morrison's foreign policy agenda.

I thank the Executive Director of the Lowy Institute, Michael Fullilove, for this opportunity and Sam Roggeveen from the Institute for his assistance. I also thank Editor-in-Chief at *The Australian*, Chris Dore, and the Editor, Michelle Gunn, for their ongoing support.

Sydney, 2021

CHAPTER ONE

Morrison and Australian identity

Scott Morrison's self-identity originates with the arrival of Europeans in Australia. One of the 11 ships of the First Fleet was the *Scarborough* with its 208 convicts aboard, including William Roberts, who hailed from the tiny village of St Keverne near Cornwall and was transported for stealing five-and-a-half pounds of yarn worth nine shillings. Arriving on 26 January 1788, Roberts began a new life. He would become fifth great-grandfather to Australia's thirtieth prime minister.

The Second Fleet of six ships arrived to a near starving colony on 3 June 1790 with one of its ships, the *Neptune*, bringing 78 female convicts, including Kezia Brown, a gardeners' labourer transported for stealing clothing. A few years later, Brown married Roberts at St Philips Anglican Church in Sydney, the oldest Anglican Church parish in the country. They raised a family in what is now Western Sydney. Brown would become Morrison's fifth great-grandmother. She and Roberts are buried together at St Matthews in Windsor.[1]

Morrison traces his ancestry to both the First and Second Fleets. On Australia Day, he honours not just the national day, but the inception of his family line. His family narrative runs in parallel with the narrative of European settlement on the Australian continent. This vests Morrison with an ancestral claim on the contradiction at Australia's heart – pride in European civilisation and anguish at the devastation wrought on the Indigenous peoples.

At the 2007 general election, Morrison was elected to the House of Representatives for the electorate of Cook, which spans middle-class suburbs spilling onto often spectacular beaches and bays, the seat named after Captain James Cook, credited as the first European to discover and map the eastern coast of Australia in 1770. Morrison is tied to Cook by history and location in a bond that precedes by 18 years the First Fleet's arrival under Governor Arthur Phillip.

The first landing of the British on Australian soil occurred at Botany Bay (Kamay) on the Kurnell peninsula headland, now a conspicuous feature in Morrison's seat. On 29 April 1770, Cook's ship the HMS *Endeavour* anchored in the bay for eight days with the initial landing party challenged by two natives. 'James Cook was a man before his time,' Morrison said in his first speech to the House of Representatives. 'Against a backdrop of brutality and ignorance, he displayed an amazing empathy and respect for his own crew and the people and lands he visited. He should be revered as one of the most significant figures in our national history.'[2]

For Morrison, the modern Australian story begins with Cook, the navigator of the Pacific. The next phase follows with the First Fleet under Phillip. The imaginative force of these events lives with Morrison. 'I like my history in high definition, widescreen, full, vibrant colour,' he said.[3]

This history pervades Morrison's prime-ministerial office in Parliament House, Canberra. When Morrison rises from his desk and walks beyond the foyer, he enters what he calls the 'Pacific room'. It is not an 'America room' or an 'Asian engagement room'. It is filled with photographs of Morrison with Pacific leaders: Fiji's Frank Bainimarama, PNG's James Marape, Solomon Islands' Manasseh Sogavare, New Zealand Prime Minister Jacinda Ardern and former prime minister and president of Timor-Leste Xanana Gusmao.

The room has two framed engravings of Captain Cook, a drawing of Cook's ship HMS *Resolution*, and gifts from Pacific leaders. The room is private, an expression of Morrison's identity and a declaration of neighbourhood and family.

The first Christian cleric in Australia was the Reverend Richard Johnson, a graduate of Cambridge where he absorbed evangelical principles. His 1786 appointment as chaplain of New South Wales owed much to the influence of the charismatic parliamentarian and opponent of the slave trade William Wilberforce, who wanted to see an evangelical Christian assume the post.

Morrison has quoted Johnson's description of the miserable humanity that emerged from the Second Fleet ships after a voyage during which a quarter of the convicts died: 'They were wretched, naked, filthy, dirty, lousy and many of them utterly unable to stand or even to stir hand or foot.' Kezia Brown was among them. Morrison called it 'the worst of beginnings', yet Johnson represented the British commitment to a divine mission in the new land. It is another continuous thread, from 1788 to the present, running through Morrison's life as a Christian.[4]

In his first speech, Morrison said his parents, John and Marion Morrison, along with his grandparents, 'laid the foundation for my life'. Religion was at its heart. 'Growing up in a Christian home, I made a commitment to my faith at an early age,' Morrison said. 'My personal faith in Jesus Christ is not a political agenda. As Lincoln said, our task is not to claim whether God is on our side, but to pray earnestly that we are on His.'[5]

Explaining his family's religious journey, Morrison said his parents 'started in the Presbyterian Church and then they went Uniting, and I went to a Christian Brethren Assembly, which my brother was going to – and that's where I met Jenny – and ended up a Pentecostal, so that's quite a journey.' Morrison said an alternative life as a religious, not a political, minister had been a 'pretty close' call for him.

It was faith that his parents transmitted to Morrison, and faith that led Morrison to Jenny Warren. Morrison was 11 years old when they met. 'We didn't start going out till I was 16,' he said. Apart from a two-week break, they have been together ever since. They married in 1990 when Morrison was 21.[6]

His personal life has hardly been touched by the social and sexual revolution of the 1960s. Morrison's conservative outlook has been remarkably divorced from the tidal wave of personal progressivism that altered family life over the previous two generations.

Australian identity and cultural tradition are the driving forces in Morrison's political creed. 'I do not share the armband view of history, black or otherwise,' Morrison said. That means celebrating our achievements and acknowledging our failures 'at least in equal measure'.[7] Morrison said that 'when you trace your family history back to when settlement began', then you feel a bond with the story of European engagement with Indigenous Australians 'in all its history and its brutality and dispossession'.[8]

Yet, for Morrison, the 'wonder' of Australia is that hardship and cruelty bequeathed a nation that is decent, fair and prosperous. He sees Australia – not the United States – as the model democracy. His family ties anchor him to the redemptive transformation that saw a collection of convicts and military officers seed a new democracy.

Welcoming people to a citizenship ceremony on 26 January 2019, Prime Minister Morrison drew the link between these newest Australians and his personal ties with the oldest European Australians. 'I am glad William and Kezia made the journey,' he said. 'And I'm glad you have, too.'

At this ceremony, he quoted historian and former Liberal politician David Kemp on Australia as 'the ideal place to experiment with such radical ideas as broad individual liberty and equality, universal education, freedom of the press, freedom of religion, a new land without slavery, the rule of law, the class-less society, private enterprise and later, the political and social equality of men and women.'[9]

Morrison's sense of Australian identity is buried deep in a thicket of family, nation, history and location. This is how he sees and operates in the world – these things are real, not abstractions. They coalesce in a conclusion: faith in the Australian project and belief in the Australian character. This fount of identity lies at the heart of his dealings with the world – whether that is with America, China, Japan or India, or chairing the National Security Committee of Cabinet (NSC).

In his 2017 book *The Road to Somewhere*, British journalist David Goodhart described the fundamental cultural divide in Britain – and the West at large – as being between the 'anywheres' and the 'somewheres'.[10] The former are mobile, elitist, cosmopolitan, successful decision-makers, global in mentality, liberated from traditions of faith, flag and family. The latter – who prioritise place, so typically live near where they were raised – are socially conservative, value tradition, habits, nation, religion and tribal ties, and are often accused by progressives of being irrational and reactionary. As a foreign policy prime minister, Morrison is obligated to be a globalist, yet in his essence he is a 'somewhere' leader.

This suggests a foreign policy anchored to national identity, conservative values and domestic political needs – and that is what Morrison delivers.

Morrison said his faith is not a 'political agenda' – an essential qualification given leaders operating in the temporal world can never match biblical injunctions. However, he nominates William Wilberforce and South Africa's Desmond Tutu as Christian leaders who 'transformed their nations and, indeed, the world'.

'By following the convictions of their faith, they established and reinforced the principles of our liberal democracy upon which our own nation is built,' Morrison said. He draws the nexus between his faith and liberal democracy. Morrison's faith informs his view of the world.[11]

The proposition here is not that Morrison has a superior morality or that morality governs his politics. It is that he brings his sense of Australian identity, conservative tradition and values to his formulation of foreign policy. He does not wear them on his sleeve, since that is not the Australian way. But as Prime Minister, dealing with the world, Morrison carries his identity and values before him in three distinct ways.

First, he anchors his foreign policy on Australian identity. Everything begins and ends with identity. Australia, he asserts, is a strong nation, his constant refrain being: we know who we are; we know what we believe; we know whose side we are on.

Second, in his ties closest to home – his relations with Pacific leaders – Morrison frames his policy as an extension of family values. Families can disagree but possess a shared bond.

Third, Morrison sees the contest between China and the West not just in power terms, but as a moral encounter between China's quasi-capitalist authoritarianism and the Enlightenment's legacy of liberal democracy. For him, it is a competition based on power and morals.

Morrison became Prime Minister in August 2018 after an abrupt party crisis that produced a surprise result. He assumed the highest office just 11 years after entering the parliament and, in the view of many, before he was fully prepared. He was steeped in neither foreign policy experience nor international diplomatic practice. Indeed, such inexperience suggested an amateur in the field, raising the possibility that something might go seriously wrong.

But Morrison arrived with attitude. This was a deeply grounded political leader with entrenched views about Australia, sure of his own identity and carrying passionate beliefs. He would inject them into Australian foreign policy amid a world in transition.

CHAPTER TWO

A world transformed

From the beginning of his prime ministership, Scott Morrison was driven by the dynamic of a world being transformed. He felt his task as Prime Minister was to manage unprecedented changes in the established order.

A new era of ideological and strategic rivalry was consuming US–China relations. The Indo-Pacific risked becoming a focus of great power competition. China was challenging the United States, which had been Australia's senior alliance partner for nearly 70 years. Within America, there was waning support for the US global leadership role, while a more assertive China had resorted to a range of tactics to expand its influence, including militarisation of artificial islands in the South China Sea. The opportunities from the digital age had a downside in the explosion of cyber interference measures and high-tech national competition. The economic dividends from globalisation were under assault in Western democracies for the inequalities they had bequeathed. Within China and America, events were reshaping global politics, notably the 2018 move by China's President Xi Jinping to make himself leader in perpetuity and Donald Trump's 2016 presidential victory, pledging a more inward-looking and protectionist America in a shift away from generations of US leadership.

In October 2019, Morrison introduced himself as a foreign policy thinker when delivering the annual Lowy Lecture to an elite audience at the Sydney Town Hall. Morrison said, 'As a politician, my instincts and passions have always been domestic. Despite my activity of the past year, I am not one who naturally seeks out summits and international platforms. But as Prime Minister, you must always be guided by the national interest.'[12] Yet, belying his humility, after 14 months in office Morrison had embraced a global outlook sweeping in its framing if not yet fully formed.

'We are living in a world in transition that former US treasury secretary Hank Paulson has described as "an unusually delicate moment in time",' Morrison told the Sydney Town Hall audience.

'A new economic and political order is still taking shape. We have entered a new era of strategic competition.'[13]

This view pre-dated the main retaliatory trade actions China would impose on Australia, and the COVID-19 pandemic. Yet the sheer magnitude of the disruptions Morrison listed – technological, strategic, societal, cultural and economic – demanded a multifaceted response. Foreign and domestic policy would be more interlinked than ever. This was a complex world of menacing disruption.

Nine months later, courtesy of COVID-19, a global recession and China's coercive campaign against Australia, Morrison's assessments had hardened into a dire view of the global outlook. In July 2020, Morrison launched the Defence Strategic Update and a revamped defence posture to meet the disruption caused by China's muscle flexing. Resorting to language not used by an Australian prime minister for decades and employing some contentious historical analogies, Morrison said:

We have been a favoured isle with many natural advantages for many decades, but we have not seen the conflation of global, economic and strategic uncertainty now being experienced here in Australia in our region since the existential threat we faced when the global and regional order collapsed in the 1930s and 1940s. That is a sobering thought and it's something I have reflected on quite a lot lately as we've considered the dire economic circumstances we face. That period of the 1930s has been something I have been revisiting on a very regular basis and when you connect both the economic challenges and the global uncertainty, it can be very haunting.

But not overwhelming. It requires a response. Now we must face that reality, understanding that we have moved into a new and less benign strategic area, one in which the institutions of patterns of cooperation that have benefited our prosperity and security for decades are now under increasing – and I would suggest almost irreversible – strain.[14]

After listing the range of regional tensions, Morrison said, 'The risk of miscalculation and even conflict is heightening. Regional military modernisation is occurring at an unprecedented rate.' He announced a new ten-year funding model for defence, extending beyond the Coalition's previous pledge to reach two per cent of GDP. 'We've crashed through that,' Morrison said, stating that the defence budget 'has reached momentum again' and that 'we're not going to be constrained by two per cent'.[15]

Former head of the Department of Defence Dennis Richardson said, 'China is the obvious backdrop. That doesn't need to be explicitly stated. It is fully understood.' The then defence minister Linda Reynolds, in an echo of Morrison, said, 'The world we all grew up in is no more.'[16]

There were two risks with such language. First, that the response would not match the alarm being raised. Second, invoking the 1930s invited false analogies. What Morrison meant to convey was that, unlike the 1930s in Australia, he would not let defence preparedness be sacrificed to an economic downturn. He sought to repudiate the follies of the 1930s, a point he clarified at the time: 'Many others in a crisis like this might have looked for an excuse to step back [on defence]. Not us.'[17]

The following month in his August 2020 virtual address to the Aspen Security Forum, Morrison reinforced his theme, quoting US analyst Robert Kagan, who called for the United States to maintain its internationalist posture to prevent a descent into the law of the jungle. 'The liberal rules and norms of what has been known as the American Century are under assault,' the Prime Minister said. Speaking to an American audience, Morrison's theme was that the danger was coalescing in the Indo-Pacific, where Australia lived. The region had become 'the epicentre of strategic competition'. He continued:

> Tensions over territorial claims are growing. The pace of military modernisation is unprecedented. Democratic nations face new threats from foreign interference. Cyberattacks are increasing in frequency and sophistication. Disinformation is being used to manipulate free societies. And economic coercion is increasingly employed as a tool of statecraft.[18]

For Morrison, Beijing was the central disrupter, the anti-status quo power, posing a unique challenge: an authoritarian state with a high-tech, quasi-capitalist economy, unwilling to abide by established norms, ready to break rules, defy international rulings and threaten neighbouring jurisdictions while parading its efficiency as an alternative to liberal democracy.

But China's story was not occurring in isolation. Since the Global Financial Crisis a decade earlier, both the United States and China had ceased to be status quo powers. Both nations increasingly sought changes in the global system. Xi Jinping wanted China's economic weight recognised, and signalled that China would not just accept international norms devised by others. American sentiment, climaxing with Donald Trump's victory, was that the liberal economic order had been exploited by China against the United States and that the US alliance system saw America bearing too much of the burden and its allies carrying too many of the benefits.

Morrison's diagnosis – though not necessarily his solution – was widely shared in the foreign policy and intelligence community. Allan Gyngell, formerly an officer at the Department of Foreign Affairs and Trade (DFAT), an adviser to Prime Minister Paul Keating, and director-general of the Office of National Assessments (ONA), said, 'There is no doubt in my mind that the post-Second World War order that suited Australia so much has come to an end. It's not being challenged. It's not changing. It's over.'[19]

Richard Maude, the principal author of the 2017 Foreign Policy White Paper and a former DFAT deputy secretary and director-general of ONA, said, 'Morrison inherited a foreign policy already beginning to adapt to a world in transformation. More change is coming. Morrison now faces a steady stream of consequential policy decisions as the old world order unravels and US–China competition ramps up.'[20]

Reflecting on her time as DFAT secretary and former ambassador to China, Frances Adamson said, 'The values, systems and standing of the developed world are being challenged. The West's advantage in economic, military and technological power is ebbing. The international order is being remade and there are big agendas ahead for Australia.'[21]

The organising principle of Morrison's foreign policy was to influence, as much as possible, the new global order that would emerge. In essence, he was building upon the 2017 Foreign Policy White Paper, with its theme of a contested world order, a weakening of multilateral institutions and rivalry in the Indo-Pacific, where China's power and influence was 'growing to match, and in some cases exceed, that of the United States'.[22]

By 2020, the principles that would govern Morrison's approach were clearly articulated. Interviewed for this Paper, Morrison described these principles under a trio of headings: sovereign capability, Australian agency, and the struggle for liberal democracy against China's authoritarian model.

These labels highlight a potential contradiction in Morrison: he is both a realist and an idealist. Above all, Morrison sees nation states as the 'building blocks' of the global order and 'sovereign capability' as the decisive means to protect the national interest. 'At all times, we must be true to our values and the protection of our own sovereignty,' Morrison said, enunciating his golden rule.[23]

For Morrison, nation state sovereignty is a lived experience. It shapes everything he touches and feels in political life. In his first portfolio as minister for Immigration and Border Protection, Morrison directed one of the most important sovereignty projects in Australia's history – the whole-of-government Operation Sovereign Borders, which terminated the flow of asylum seeker boats to the continent.

Its success owed much to Morrison's planning and determination and earnt him the lasting enmity of progressives. In delivering on this objective, Morrison revealed qualities that would make him a potential candidate for prime minister.

As treasurer, his concept of state sovereignty matured – no longer confined to physical borders, it also encompassed fiscal prudence, investor confidence and inclusive economic growth. His thinking was refined further sitting in the NSC during the Turnbull government, assessing data on hostile activity via cyberattack, foreign interference and high-tech espionage. At every stage, Morrison's ministerial experience deepened his concept of sovereignty protection.

By 2020, battling against the pandemic, Morrison had expanded 'sovereign capability' to an all-encompassing principle. Economist Chris Richardson said COVID-19 had exposed nations at their weakest point.[24] Morrison would have agreed. He began to talk about 'resilience', by which he meant all-round strength. There were many elements in Morrison's 'resilience' matrix: an effective health system, a stable democracy, economic recovery, a solid defence industry, supply chains, cybersecurity, technology, energy and manufacturing capability, national disaster resources and the human and material infrastructure to succeed in an age of risk and uncertainty.[25]

He presented the 2020 Defence Strategic Update and Force Structure Plan as fundamental to sovereignty. His decision to establish an Australian vaccine production capability at biotech company CSL in Melbourne was an example of sovereign capability, as was the $300 billion–plus emergency fiscal policy to combat recession and preserve economic resilience.

In Morrison's view, sovereignty is tied to identity. Sovereign capability enables Australia to live by its own values. This is a subject on which he is passionate. 'Sovereignty means self-respect, freedom to be who we are,' Morrison says. 'We will never surrender this. Never. Ever. Everything my government does is designed to build our national resilience and protect our sovereignty, our freedom, our values and our independence.'[26]

In a more dangerous world, Morrison sees sovereignty as under threat. For him, this is not just a national security challenge – the task is to defend Australian identity. Sovereign capability, he told the author, is the essential condition to surviving as the nation 'we want to be', and that means being able to 'act in accordance with your character'.[27] Without sovereign capability, he said, 'we can't do much'.

The risk in this emphasis on sovereignty and identity is seeing dangers as an existential challenge. Threats vary in terms of the risk they pose to national assets and the limits they impose on decision-making. But most threats fall short of a serious risk to national sovereignty and identity. By the emphasis he places on identity, Morrison runs the risk of over-reacting to adverse actions taken by other nations against Australia. Yet it has become fundamental to his response to China. At the core of Morrison's thinking lies an existential risk to Australia.

Morrison is prone to emotional overreaction in defence of Australia's reputation. Witness his furious 2019 response to the ludicrous comments by Turkish President Recep Tayyip Erdoğan, who said anyone coming to Turkey with anti-Muslim sentiments would be sent back in coffins 'like their grandfathers' at Gallipoli. Morrison summoned the Turkish ambassador and at a press conference called for the remarks to be withdrawn, saying they insulted 'the memory of the Anzacs' and violated the pledge enshrined in stone at Gallipoli by Turkey's contemporary founder, Mustafa Kemal Atatürk. On another occasion, he called a press conference demanding an apology and the removal of a repugnant tweet by a senior Chinese official showing a doctored picture of an Australian soldier threatening to slit the throat of an Afghan child. Beijing refused both demands.

Peter Varghese, former secretary of DFAT and director-general of ONA, says, 'Morrison is giving sovereignty a deeper practical and policy meaning. This arises from the times – the pandemic, China's behaviour and geostrategic tensions. There is a new language about protection, self-reliance and domestic supply chains.'[28]

Morrison's emphasis on sovereign capability is a hedge against further disintegration of the rules-based multilateral order. He governs at a time when globalisation is in retreat, multilateral institutions are weakened and economic nationalism is rising. Morrison has been equivocal about which side of this debate he supports – he has attacked the notion of 'negative globalism', while supporting the liberal trade system and seeking better international co-operation on pandemic management. In his speeches, Morrison presents himself as a realist who believes

Australia must 'do more in its own right' in today's world and fears that without greater self-sufficiency the nation may be left exposed.

Morrison's second operating principle is agency – maximising Australia's ability to shape the Indo-Pacific, the region it shares. 'I have been impressed by the urgency of doing,' he says. 'Being willing is not enough; we must do.'[29] Morrison's character is that of a compulsive political activist. He is always on the move, talking, travelling, doing. Indeed, many of Morrison's tactical mistakes stem from his compulsion to respond too quickly.

He is not a leader for retreat or isolation. Morrison's abiding concern is to build coalitions of shared interest. 'Internationally, we need to project, build, develop and leverage our agency,' he says. 'Now, that agency is leveraged in all sorts of ways through our alliances, our partnerships, our alignments, principally with those who share the values and character that we do as a country.' In a high-tech age, he wants Australia to have a multitude of connections, what he calls 'influence built on national assets'.[30]

His concept of agency encompasses the US alliance, the Five Eyes intelligence-sharing arrangement, the Pacific Step-up, the Reciprocal Access Agreement with Japan, the Quad (Quadrilateral Security Dialogue between Australia, the United States, Japan and India), the Comprehensive and Progressive Agreement for Trans-Pacific Partnership on trade (CPTPP), the long-standing relationship with the Association of Southeast Asian Nations (ASEAN), attendance at G7 summits, membership of the G20, and involvement in multilateral institutions and in regional and bilateral free trade agreements. These tangible proofs of agency stand in a strong line of Australian diplomatic tradition.

The ultimate purpose is to work with other sovereign nations to deliver an Indo-Pacific region where countries engage freely without coercion. Morrison has a view of the region, not just a view of the US alliance or the China challenge. He says Australia and regional nations 'are not just bystanders' to US–China competition. 'Japan, India, the Republic of Korea, the countries of Southeast Asia, Indonesia, Malaysia, Singapore, Vietnam and the Pacific all have agency, choices to make, parts to play and, of course, so does Australia.'[31]

This means ensuring the Indo-Pacific does not lose control of its own destiny and become a mere staging ground for US–China confrontation. 'We are all participants with agency and purpose,' Morrison said in 2020. 'We can shape our destiny, individually and collectively.' The aim is to avoid a Hobbesian disorder across the Indo-Pacific. 'It's not just China and the United States that will determine whether our region stays on the path for free and open trade, investment and the cooperation that has under-pinned stability and prosperity,' he said. Southeast Asia need not succumb to client status to China, and countries with heft – Japan, India, Australia and Indonesia – can exercise influence and find common cause. Nation states, Morrison says, must prove their worth and show they 'are not simply boats being tossed around in an angry sea'.[32]

He believes that the twenty-first century great powers have a responsibility to manage their competition short of a disastrous military conflict. 'Greater latitude will be required from the world's largest powers to accommodate the individual interests of their partners and allies,' Morrison said. 'We all need a bit more room to move.' Morrison believes the global order is always imperfect, but that the Indo-Pacific can be secured free of coercion by nations working in alliances, collaborations and partnerships of mutual self-interest.[33] Richard Maude says, 'This is his most important foreign policy objective.'[34]

While Morrison does not believe the United States is the sole answer, his sense of realpolitik means he sees the US contribution to the Indo-Pacific as essential. America, he insists, must stay committed.

Morrison says the rise of China makes it imperative 'to build a durable strategic balance in the Indo-Pacific', a goal unachievable without America, and central to Australia's agency.

China's campaign of trade coercion against Australia sharpened Morrison's mind in two directions: it affirmed his quest for the United States to remain involved in the region to limit bullying by other great powers; and it reinforced his efforts to pursue a rules-based order to facilitate economic and trade development. China's trade retaliation against Australia, therefore, cannot be just a bilateral issue. As far as Morrison is concerned, it is a global test case of whether the international system will be governed by rules or by the law of the jungle.

While usually shunning theoretical approaches to foreign policy, Morrison has drawn on the work of Australian scholar Hedley Bull, a professor at both the Australian National University and Oxford, describing Bull's *The Anarchical Society* as 'one of the most influential' books on global politics of the past century. Bull argued that despite the chaotic nature of global politics, it is composed of nations capable of forming 'a society of states' when they recognise a 'common set of rules' and institutions despite their rivalries. This is the light of hope that runs through the darkest of Morrison's disruption ruminations.

In short, Morrison's conception of Australian agency is geared to both power and values. He sees a strategic balance as essential in the Indo-Pacific, along with a rules-based order that respects international law and peaceful dispute resolution. By Morrison's calculations, both dimensions are necessary to secure Australia's future.

In 2021, his preoccupation with building Australia's influence became an activist obsession. This was reflected in two events. The first was US President Joe Biden's initiative to give the Quad momentum by inaugurating its first meeting at leaders' level. The second was former finance minister Mathias Cormann's elevation to secretary-general of the 38 member Paris-based Organisation for Economic Cooperation and Development (OECD), overcoming a highly competitive field of candidates.

Biden's move on the Quad revealed an alignment with Morrison's aspirations. It was exactly what Morrison had sought in his Indo-Pacific diplomacy, though the initiative was Biden's. Morrison saw it as vindication of a sustained chapter in Australian diplomacy, pursued by himself and Foreign Minister Marise Payne.

The Cormann appointment was different – it constituted the single most intense diplomatic campaign conducted by Morrison since he became

Prime Minister. It began in May 2020, several months before Cormann's candidature was announced in September. Morrison's office reports that, from start to finish, the Prime Minister personally lobbied 55 heads of government and senior figures on Cormann's behalf. Cormann conducted his own intense campaign and was advantaged by his credentials as a long-term finance minister, his connection to the Asia-Pacific and his fluency in several European languages.

The OECD post is not an appointment of strategic significance. The organisation produces research and advocates for policy reform across the spectrum of global challenges – economic growth, social equity, climate change, tax and productivity.[35] But for Morrison, the Cormann success had extra meaning – at a time when Australia was under intense pressure from China, it proved the capacity of Morrison's diplomacy and of Australia's credibility. Typically, Morrison oversold the results. But that reflected a prime minister running a high-stakes diplomatic campaign in which his personal involvement was conspicuous. With a note of vindication, he told the author, 'Where do we put the effort in? Massively into sovereign capability, massively into levering our agency.'[36]

The third element of Morrison's framework is the newest, springing directly from his perception of the China challenge. Morrison believes the world faces a contest between liberal democratic and authoritarian models of governance. He sees the rivalry between the United States and China as unprecedented because the two largest economies and most powerful states confront each other as champions of incompatible models of political organisation and civilisational values. Morrison believes Australia must play a leadership role in the Indo-Pacific as an advocate of liberal-democratic values and rejects the notion that China's challenge merely relates to external policy.

In Morrison's view, the nexus is irrefutable: if liberal democracy is weakened, the norms of the regional and global order will no longer be shaped by democratic values. He argues this would constitute a dangerous departure from the post-Second World War order when American leadership was critical in helping to establish multilateral norms. Morrison says freedom of thought and expression, inalienable human rights, free and open markets, free flow of capital and ideas, freedom of choice and freedom from oppression and coercion have 'never been more important'.

'And they are under threat,' he says.

The great risk now is that this liberal-based world order will become compromised by a relativist agenda that says all systems are good and we're all members and our outlooks are all as good as the other. How can you have a credible rules-based order that is effectively over-sighted by nations that don't have a rules-based order in their own polities, in their own countries?

Morrison expressed these sentiments in 2020, but by 2021 they had become distinctly elevated, coinciding with the arrival of President Biden who propounded – at least initially – a similar message. Morrison told the author: 'What we want to achieve and preserve is a global order and strategic balance that favours freedom.'[37]

Reflecting on Morrison's theme, Richard Maude says:

I think it is inevitable that our foreign policy will be more influenced by system competition with China. While China does not export its model as such, it promotes its model as superior – based on efficiency and delivery in dealing with and extending credit to a wide range of nations. China is bringing this model to our shores, one way or another. It cannot be ignored.[38]

In a March 2021 speech, Morrison gave his strongest expression to this idea:

There has never been a more important time, I think, since the Second World War, where Australia has to stand and lead the way amongst liberal democracies, as we have before, in standing up for liberal democracy. This is the great polarisation that our world is at risk of moving towards. Liberal democracies, authoritarian autocracies, this is what the four Quad leaders gathered together to speak about.[39]

Five months earlier in his UK address, Morrison had hammered the same theme: 'This is a moment for concerted leadership and action by like-minded liberal democracies.'[40]

This constitutes a significant departure for Australian policy, based for many decades on the belief that in dealing with the Asia-Pacific the national interest cannot be defined by whether nations are democracies. The long-established democracies are in the Atlantic zone of North America and Europe, not Asia. Seeking to rally Asian nations around a liberal democratic agenda is problematic for Australia. However, it is not apparent that Morrison has actually taken this message to the region, and indeed he has also advanced relations with non-democratic states, notably Vietnam.

Peter Varghese says, 'While it is becoming fashionable to promote the struggle of liberal democracy versus the authoritarian state, I doubt this will become the key fault line of the future. I don't think this is how most nations in our region see the situation.'[41]

Morrison's sense of identity and his fidelity to the Western liberal tradition lie at the core of his foreign policy project. He says China's engagement in a competition of 'systems' cannot be ignored by liberal democracies. The challenge must be met. Yet, as Richard Maude says, 'A global alliance bridging North America, Asia and Europe to defend democracy and push back against Chinese coercion, even a loose and uneven one, is striking new territory for Australian foreign policy.'[42]

This suggests a difference in foreign policy temperament and outlook between Morrison and John Howard. Howard teamed up with US President George W. Bush over the Iraq war, but his justification for Australia's entry was limited – disarming Iraq – and did not embrace Bush's goals of regime change and bringing liberal-democratic nation building to Iraq. In foreign policy, Howard was rarely ideological and typically suspicious of American rhetorical grandeur about liberal democracy.

How far Biden pursues his democratic narrative remains to be seen. But Biden's language and philosophy are those of a great power. Morrison is pushing Australia into new and more ideological territory by championing liberal democracy. The extent to which this remains a rhetorical aspiration or involves diplomatic action remains to be seen.

However, the three principles that guide Morrison's foreign policy – sovereignty, agency and liberal democracy – have the potential, if pursued robustly, to significantly diverge from the Australian foreign policy tradition.

CHAPTER THREE

The rise of national security

Scott Morrison would preside over a transformation in foreign policy that had erupted during the Turnbull prime ministership: the rise in policy influence of the national security agencies. This had been an evolving story since the Coalition's return to office in 2013, with Morrison a participant as immigration minister and then treasurer.

So on becoming Prime Minister in 2018, he represented an interesting duality – a diplomatic novice but already a proven national security guardian. Calling Morrison a 'hawkish' prime minister missed the point. His formative experiences in the Turnbull cabinet lay in national security, encompassing external and internal policy. This was a comfortable fit given Morrison's emphasis on sovereignty protection. And it had the convenient bonus that national security was usually tied to domestic political advantage – it won media and public support.

Foreign policy and national security veteran Peter Varghese describes the transformation:

One decisive change in the Turnbull–Morrison period has been the rise in influence of the intelligence agencies. This coincides with a new agenda: the intensification of national security, China's influence operations and sovereignty concerns. A threshold has been crossed with the intelligence agencies now having a direct policy impact in a way we have probably not seen before. These agencies have enjoyed vast expansions in their budgets, while DFAT has struggled. Within the system, national security is more important and diplomacy is less important. Follow the money – that reveals the changed priorities. DFAT has been cut because successive governments see no political cost in doing so. The foundation stone in Justice Hope's review of the security services was the need to separate intelligence assessment from policymaking. But this is now being eroded.[43]

Analysis by the Lowy Institute over many years has documented the funding squeeze on DFAT. Projected real spending in 2024 will be less than in 2014, a time when the budget had already shrunk. The Lowy Institute says Australia has one of the smallest diplomatic networks among developed nations.[44] Meanwhile, the combined budget for the nation's ten intelligence and security agencies has soared to beyond $2 billion and 7,000 staff.[45]

Director-General of Security, Mike Burgess, asked whether he agreed that prime ministers now spend more time dealing with intelligence than in the past, said:

> I would [agree]. I think the world's circumstances dictate their demands for intelligence . . . at a time of great power competition and a geopolitical circumstance that is complex, challenging and changing, intelligence informs government and decision-makers and allows them to make informed decisions . . . The Prime Minister [Scott Morrison] is demanding in terms of his intelligence needs and a great reader of the intelligence that his agencies give him. I think Malcolm Turnbull had more of an interest in how that sausage was made.[46]

National security had become fundamental to Morrison's political character before he became Prime Minister. As minister for Immigration and then treasurer, he sat in the engine room of security decision-making – the National Security Committee of Cabinet (NSC). Neither Malcolm Turnbull nor Tony Abbott had the benefit of such experience before becoming Prime Minister. As a consequence, Morrison was more familiar with the security environment than either Turnbull or Abbott when they assumed office.

Sitting in the NSC, Morrison was involved to varying degrees in the Turnbull government's security-based pushback against China. There were four flash points in this process: the 2015 decision by the Northern Territory government to lease the Port of Darwin to a Chinese-owned company for $506 million, triggering a furious domestic backlash that lasted a number of years; the 2016 veto, with Morrison as treasurer, of the NSW Liberal government's sale of 50.4 per cent of Ausgrid, the largest electricity network in Australia, to two bidders, a Chinese state-owned company and a Hong Kong-listed company; the 2017 passage of unprecedented foreign interference laws, largely provoked by intelligence data about China's activities in Australia; and the banning of Chinese company Huawei and other high-risk vendors from Australia's 5G network, the single most important security decision of the Turnbull years, announced on the second-last full day of his prime ministership.

Turnbull was the ideal prime minister to oversee this policy revolution. He arrived with a business mindset that was pro-China, and he was the most technologically savvy prime minister in Australia's history; vital qualities in ensuring a credible transformation in policy.

Turnbull and Morrison were allies on the Huawei policy, yet Morrison was keen to put his own stamp on the decision after he became Prime Minister. The decision was finally taken by the NSC on 14 August 2018, but announced on 23 August in a joint statement by Morrison as acting Home Affairs Minister and Communications Minister Mitch Fifield. The statement was generic and did not mention Huawei (or ZTE, a smaller Chinese tech company), but the Chinese had been informed of the ban by the Australian government.

'We knew there would be risks with China's response,' Turnbull said.

> My aim was to give Beijing the opportunity to let the ball go through to the keeper. We took the decision, informed the Chinese and decided there would be a joint announcement by the Home Affairs minister and the Communications minister. It was agreed the PM and Foreign minister would say nothing at the time.[47]

Turnbull further stated:

> We gave the Americans a heads up, we gave the Chinese in Beijing a heads up, we gave Huawei and ZTE a heads up, we gave everyone who had an interest a heads up in advance, so there were no surprises . . . It was all carefully orchestrated. What was the reason for that? We didn't want to raise any hackles or angst.[48]

What was not orchestrated, however, was the Liberal leadership crisis. With Home Affairs Minister Peter Dutton resigning after his failed leadership challenge against Turnbull, Morrison assumed Dutton's ministry in an acting capacity, which meant a Morrison–Fifield announcement. Morrison subsequently put immense weight on the fact the announcement had come under his ministerial letterhead.

Asked if he felt a sense of ownership of the Huawei decision, Morrison said, 'Yes, in many ways I was its architect.' Asked how, Morrison commented, 'It was my decision.' Morrison said that within the NSC he had begun to focus on security issues, aware that 'technology's a risk, quantum computing's a risk, data centres are a risk'.[49] Morrison had run hard against Huawei and said the recommendation had come from him and Fifield.[50] Yet the claim that it was Morrison's decision seems a manifest exaggeration, given the sequence.

Morrison's comments, however, reveal that the Huawei decision has become a benchmark for the national security credentials of individual ministers. Over the years, many ministers and some officials have wanted to enjoy its lustre. The decision has come to be seen as an example of Australia's technical capacity, courage in defying China and leadership in showing other nations how to protect their 5G networks.

Obviously, it was a collective NSC decision. At every stage, Turnbull had been intimately involved and, more than any other minister, his imprint as prime minister was on the decision. Turnbull had studied the technological issues and had commissioned then Australian Signals Directorate (ASD) chief Mike Burgess to determine whether a secure method existed to allow Huawei into the system.

Burgess was the pivotal official in Australia's single most important security-related decision in years. Indeed, it is hard to see this decision being taken without him. Nothing better illustrates the rise in policy impact of the security agencies.

Turnbull's starting position had been to find a way to allow Huawei to participate in the 5G network. Burgess said the relevant question for his analysis became, 'What would you need to do to manage that risk?' Burgess told the author, 'That was a very thorough process based on the capability of the Australian Signals Directorate . . . In the end I, as director-general of ASD, formed the view that despite the large number of mitigation steps you could put in place, you could not mitigate the risks successfully.'[51]

It was Burgess's advice that convinced Turnbull not to take the risk. Turnbull had wanted to know if he could say yes and, if not, he wanted to know why the answer must be no. In the end, Turnbull went through the analysis line by line. Given Burgess's technical advice, Turnbull had to veto Huawei.[52] The decision was the ultimate example of how technical advice from the national security bureaucracy left a prime minister with no viable option but to accept the recommendation.

'Our decision on 5G was the first formal ban of Huawei and ZTE in the world,' Turnbull said. It was the subject of his final phone call as Prime Minister with Donald Trump. The president, Turnbull said, 'was both impressed and a little surprised'.[53]

Long before Huawei, Morrison's security focus had been entrenched. As treasurer, Morrison seeded far-reaching changes in foreign investment policy, allowing for more severe restrictions on

Chinese investment in Australia. The final stage was the reconceptualisation of foreign investment policy developed in the June 2020 announcement by Treasurer Josh Frydenberg. This saw foreign investment being evaluated in terms of security advantage, not just economic return. It increased the treasurer's powers and authorised a $0 threshold for scrutiny of any investment with security sensitivity. By this stage, a policy revolution was well advanced – about 80 per cent of foreign investment approvals by value had conditions of one sort or another attached.[54]

The first such foreign investment 'wake up' call for Morrison came over the Port of Darwin sale. This followed consultation by the Northern Territory government with the Foreign Investment Review Board (FIRB) and the Department of Defence on its proposed sale to the Chinese-owned company Landbridge, a subsidiary of the Shandong Landbridge Group, a private company based in China. Under the Act, the federal government was not required to give formal approval to the 99-year lease proposal for part of the port because the law exempted assets owned by state and territory governments.[55]

However, the lease was assessed by the NSC and met no objection. One participant said,

'No concern was expressed by any minister, by any departmental head or by any security agency chief.' It was seen as a done deal, but the Americans were deeply unhappy. President Barack Obama complained to Turnbull in November 2015 that the US government had found out about the lease from a media report. From its inception, the decision was attacked as a major security oversight.

Morrison, as treasurer, wanted no repeat of this incident. He changed the foreign takeover regulations to ensure the exemption that had applied to Darwin Port was removed. The treasurer was authorised to assess security issues across a wide range of investment assets including airports, ports, electricity, gas, roads, railways and telecommunications. Morrison appointed to the FIRB a public servant deeply versed in security issues, former diplomat David Irvine, a previous chief of both the Australian Security Intelligence Organisation (ASIO) and the Australian Secret Intelligence Service (ASIS). The treasurer was taking out national security insurance.

Asked in April 2021 if he would have stopped the Darwin Port decision, Morrison said, 'I think I would. Let me be more clear – yes, which is why I changed the rules afterwards.'[56] Later in 2021, the Morrison government, with Peter Dutton as Defence Minister, announced it was reviewing the

Darwin Port decision, seeking new advice from the Department of Defence and giving itself a fresh option to either confirm or revise the earlier decision.

In 2016, a more significant foreign investment proposal had come before the FIRB: the proposed investment in Ausgrid by a huge Chinese government-owned company, State Grid, and a privately owned Hong Kong-listed company. State Grid was an established investor in Australian gas and utilities, approved by both the Gillard and Abbott governments. The sale was vital to the NSW Liberal government which, under Premier Mike Baird, had won an election mandate on the issue.

The approval process was far advanced, no concerns had been raised and the 'system' was heading towards another green light. Turnbull said it was only 'at the eleventh hour, as the final treasurer's approval was required', that the jolt was delivered.[57]

Urgent advice came from the ASD under Burgess that Ausgrid was involved with telecommunication links to the most sensitive defence and intelligence facility in Australia, the Pine Gap joint installation in central Australia. Pine Gap is a component in the US global warning system of a nuclear launch by a hostile power. NSC ministers confronted the shock scenario: how would the United States respond if Australia allowed a Chinese business to own a majority share in a company supporting Pine Gap?

Confusion engulfed the NSC. Turnbull asked, 'How did we miss this the first time?' There had been a breakdown among key departments and agencies. 'I can tell you, I was furious,' Morrison said. 'I was furious with the agencies. Everyone was in their silos. I had to basically unpick the whole thing and set it right.'[58] Once again, ministers were left with the view they had no viable alternative but to act on the advice.

In his August 2016 statement, Morrison said the proposed sale was contrary to the national interest. The only explanation offered to the bidders was that security issues had arisen. No details were given. There was no appeal process. Turnbull said he and Morrison 'shared' the disappointment of the then NSW Premier, Gladys Berejiklian.

The Ausgrid story was not just a failure of process. It exposed a broken system no longer equipped to manage the emerging security challenges. Turnbull and Morrison, embarrassed by the failure, recognised that any security problem must be identified at the start of the approval process, not the end. Morrison conceded when he was subsequently in China that the Chinese had a 'legitimate' criticism and that Australia's 'no' should have come far earlier.[59]

'It highlighted the system failure,' Morrison said. 'Foreign investment now was dealing with more than just commercial transactions. It reinforced my view of having security being a key factor in the consideration.'[60] The upshot was a series of decisions to rectify the flaws.

In April 2017, Morrison announced the appointment of Irving – a security expert, not a business leader – as new chair of the FIRB, an appointment that even months earlier would have been regarded as inconceivable. In January 2017, Morrison had announced the establishment of a Critical Infrastructure Centre (CIC), its purpose being first to establish a critical asset register so the Australian government actually had a list of the assets that mattered in a security sense; and second, to build specialised knowledge of the assets in order to provide the FIRB with strong advice on the security implications of investment proposals. The immediate focus was on the areas seen as 'highest risk': water, ports, electricity, gas and telecommunications. The CIC was supported by a new law, the Security of Critical Infrastructure Act 2018.

'I was acting as a default national security agency on critical infrastructure,' Morrison said of his powers, his point being that a better process needed to be established. He called the CIC a 'very important capability within government'. In a February 2018 joint statement, Morrison and Home Affairs Minister Dutton announced all future applications for the sale of electricity assets would attract ownership restrictions or conditions for foreign buyers because in such assets the security stakes are 'higher'.[61]

The Ausgrid issue was pivotal in Morrison's security evolution. One senior official said, 'I think from this point, Morrison saw a co-equal link between security risk and economic benefit in assessing foreign investment.' Morrison told the author the lesson from the Huawei decision was that 'sovereignty needs to be maintained in every sphere', from cyber to foreign investment. He said the security challenge he faced as treasurer was 'very different from that facing my predecessors'.[62]

Morrison also drew another conclusion: that Australia's processes and systems were no longer equipped to meet evolving national security challenges. He felt the government must be ready, when required, to make fundamental changes to processes, institutions and laws to meet new challenges, notably those coming from China. This was the mindset he brought to the office of Prime Minister.

Such thinking was underpinned by the Turnbull government's 2017 decision to pass foreign interference laws, based on advice from the security agencies, the aim being to target new forms of foreign interference deemed to be 'covert, coercive or corrupt'.[63] ASIO Director-General Duncan Lewis told Turnbull and Attorney-General George Brandis that the interference threat was 'unprecedented'.

In introducing the legislation, Turnbull said ASIO had made 'significant investigative breakthroughs', but the agencies lacked 'the legislative tools they needed to act'.[64] It was some of the most forceful language Turnbull used as Prime Minister. For him, this was an act of conviction. China was the main but not the exclusive target. While Morrison was not a ministerial principal to the policy, it had his full support in the NSC.

The biggest security call under Turnbull was the Huawei ban. Turnbull, by 2018, had turned radically on China. As an insider said, 'There was no longer any discussion involving China where the glass was still half full.' For Morrison, the Huawei decision resonated with his sovereignty disposition.

Interviewed for this Paper, Mike Burgess dismissed suggestions that Australia's position on Huawei was influenced by US intelligence agencies. 'That assertion is simply wrong,' Burgess said. 'Australia led the way in identifying the risks of high-risk vendors in critical infrastructure. Our American partners were incredibly impressed with the work we did here in Australia.'[65]

Australia's decision was significant for Western nations. The United States and other countries followed Australia – a rare event. President Trump told Turnbull the United States would take the same decision.[66]

Asked whether any other security decision by an Australian government has been more influential for other nations, Burgess said:

> Probably not that I would know of in my lifetime. I say that because we were up on this risk first – what the threat and risk would be and how you would possibly manage it. We led the charge on this one. We knew where 5G would end up. It would be at the top of the nation's critical infrastructure list. If 5G wasn't running, the power grid wouldn't run, sewerage pumps wouldn't work. It would have a societal impact and the potential for a nation state to disrupt our society would be great and not possible to manage or mitigate. It was a significant decision. But it was made for Australia's interest and only for Australia . . . But there's been a ripple effect around the world.[67]

Former ASIO chief Duncan Lewis called the decision 'world leading' and said there was recognition it would have consequences for Australia: 'We all knew the decision would have wider ramifications in terms of the bilateral relationship with China and that China would see Australia's decision as a litmus test for other countries.'[68]

It is hardly a surprise that Morrison, as Prime Minister, tied himself to the Huawei decision. He was only too prepared to live with its consequences. The more Morrison saw the hardening of China's rhetoric and actions, the more convinced he became of the justification for these national security decisions. Indeed, it is tempting to think Morrison saw himself as a tougher national security guardian than Turnbull. Morrison came to the prime ministership not just to uphold Turnbull's national security revolution, but to advance it.

CHAPTER FOUR

From amateur to activist

Upon becoming Prime Minister, Scott Morrison was consumed with domestic issues but quickly accepted that he must lead on foreign policy. This need was reinforced by the loss of Julie Bishop as foreign minister, who could not stomach the post-Turnbull Liberal cabinet. Morrison had a relatively inexperienced team – Senator Marise Payne, a former Defence minister, starting as Foreign Minister and Senator Linda Reynolds as Defence Minister. Morrison was a diplomatic amateur short of experience. He did, however, possess a vital asset: he was a fast learner.

Morrison's early months reflected a prime minister under pressure. The opening Newspolls after his ascension showed Labor ahead in a catastrophic 56–44 two-party-preferred deficit, despite Morrison heading Opposition leader Bill Shorten in the personal ratings. Such pressure was reflected in every dimension of government. In foreign policy, it translated into a bizarre brew – deferring to foreign policy orthodoxy in Asia, injecting domestic priorities into foreign policy over the Jerusalem embassy relocation issue and using the Pacific Step-up to signal Morrison's personal style.

Indonesia was the first priority. Within his opening fortnight, Morrison had visited Jakarta to meet President Joko Widodo, with whom Turnbull had enjoyed good relations. The two leaders got to know each other; their talks went longer than scheduled and the personal chemistry started to build. On display was a Morrison trait. From the start, he chased strong personal connections at head-of-government level. The Morrison modus operandi, reflecting much head-of-government contemporary contact, is to stay in touch by phone and text.

In November, at his first ASEAN summit in Singapore, Morrison met among others Indian Prime Minister Narendra Modi and Singaporean Prime Minister Lee Hsien Loong, leading to personal ties that he valued deeply. He describes the Singaporean leader as 'a really great statesman', saying 'there's been more than one occasion' when he rang Lee to get his assessment of issues and received, in turn, 'very good advice'.[69] Lee, however, took a different line from Morrison on China, and in 2021 when they met in Singapore, Lee said, 'You need to work with the country . . . you can engage with it, you can negotiate with it, but it has to be a long and mutually constructive process.'[70]

In November–December 2018, Morrison attended his first G20 leaders' summit in Buenos Aires, a difficult assignment given he knew few of the leaders and was the third Australian prime minister in just over as many years. There was an embarrassing encounter with German Chancellor Angela Merkel; she was still reading a cheat sheet on Morrison, with a photograph, at the start of their session. Australia's media had a field day. A senior journalist wrote, 'Rightly or wrongly, the question on her mind seemed obvious: who's this again?'[71] Morrison called his personal relationships with leaders of the United States, Japan and India 'incredibly important'. He worked 'really hard' on relations with Boris Johnson. He described his personal links with Japan's Prime Minister Shinzo Abe as 'almost like a mentor relationship'.[72] Morrison was willing to learn from his more experienced counterparts but not necessarily take their advice.

His first diplomatic initiative was a fiasco. At the start of the final week of the October 2018 by-election campaign for Turnbull's seat of Wentworth, Morrison made the shock announcement that Australia would consider recognising Jerusalem as the capital of Israel and moving its embassy from Tel Aviv to West Jerusalem. Given the significant Jewish constituency in Wentworth, the precarious state of the campaign and the importance of the result (a defeat would threaten Morrison with minority government), the domestic consideration was apparent. Yet Morrison denied any such motive.

He said no decision had been made about recognition of the capital or moving the embassy, but the announcement was manifestly designed to raise such expectations. Morrison invoked an article written by the former ambassador to Israel, Dave Sharma, now the Liberal candidate for Wentworth, arguing this case and said he found it 'persuasive'. The impression was that Morrison was following Donald Trump, given President Trump's December 2017 decision to move the US embassy and recognise Jerusalem as the capital – a major political victory for Israel. Foreign Minister Bishop had said at the time of the US decision that Australia would not change its position and that Jerusalem's status would be subject to final negotiations between Israel and the Palestinian Authority. Morrison had been lobbied by the local Jewish community and said the issue had been raised with him 'from day one'. He said there had been no discussions with the United States on the issue and no request from Washington. 'I have made this decision,' he said.[73]

It was a classic captain's call. It showed Morrison was willing to flout diplomatic orthodoxy. It was contrary to established Liberal Party policy and the bipartisan stance of former Australian governments, and it opened the door to a shift in Australian policy on the Middle East, with implications for relations with Muslim-majority nations, Indonesia being top of the list.

Attacking the announcement, the Labor Party claimed only the United States and Guatemala had acted in this way. Shadow Foreign Minister Penny Wong said Morrison had put politics before the national interest: 'It was a decision made without going to cabinet, against long-standing advice, without consideration of the damage to our friends and neighbours.'[74] Former Australian diplomat John McCarthy, who served as ambassador and high commissioner to seven countries, mirrored much established opinion, saying, 'The Arab–Israeli question is not central to our foreign policy focus and international opinion is firmly against the position we envisage.'[75]

Indonesia was shocked and relations with Jakarta were plunged into uncertainty. The Palestinian foreign minister was in Indonesia at the time of the announcement. Indonesian Foreign Minister Retno Marsudi bluntly told Payne it would damage relations. This was serious, since Australia was awaiting Jakarta's final approval of a bilateral free trade deal. In fact, Jakarta behaved with maturity throughout the drama, sensing the policy switch was unlikely to eventuate.

The trouble for Morrison was that any policy change was unnecessary. It smacked of politics without full recognition of the consequences. It revealed the extent of Morrison's genuine pro-Israel sympathy, though this was hardly different from most past Liberal prime ministers.

Morrison was quickly forced into damage control. He commissioned Turnbull to visit Indonesia and meet Widodo. But after their meeting, Turnbull publicly warned there would be a 'very negative reaction' in Indonesia if Morrison proceeded and added that, as Prime Minister, he had assessed the embassy move option and rejected it.

The government lost the Wentworth by-election. Meanwhile, departmental secretaries were plunged into reviews and damage control, and a committee of eminent elders was selected to provide a solution. The turmoil was self-inflicted. In the end, Morrison settled on a face-saving formula endorsed by the NSC and cabinet: Australia recognised West Jerusalem as the capital, but the embassy would remain in Tel Aviv until there was a peace agreement in the distant future. Australia affirmed its support for the two-state solution. The majority of the eminent panel disagreed with the recognition of West Jerusalem as the capital, while acknowledging this was an escape clause concession for the Prime Minister.[76]

Morrison emerged from this episode with doubts about his judgment and fear that he would run a foreign policy too chained to domestic politics. Those concerns were inevitable. Sharma said he believed Morrison's initiative had been 'the right thing' at the time, but lamented it had 'become politicised in the context of a by-election'.[77]

Morrison recovered by prioritising the Pacific Step-up as his entry point into the foreign policy arena. In his November 2018 Townsville speech entitled 'Australia and the Pacific: A New Chapter', Morrison outlined the new credo.

'This is our patch,' he said of the Pacific.

This is where we have special responsibilities. We always have, we always will. We have their back and they have ours. We are connected as members of a Pacific family. It's why the first leaders I hosted in

Australia as Prime Minister have been from Solomon Islands, Fiji and Papua New Guinea.[78]

Morrison's sustained actions with the Pacific proved he was genuine; this was not a public relations exercise.

Most prime ministers outsource the bulk of Pacific diplomacy to junior ministers; it is the Australian way. But Morrison felt an emotional link and knew the Pacific was his comparative advantage in foreign policy. Morrison saw the bonds between Australia and much of the Pacific: rugby league and union, Christianity and 'family' bonds. Climate change aside, he was an ideal fit for Pacific rapport.

'As a child, I visited there quite a bit because my parents worked on cruise ships in the holidays to make extra money,' Morrison said.

I would be up there in Vanuatu – back then it was called the New Hebrides – and the Solomons. And I absolutely loved it. I returned there when I was older through my church. I developed a lot of really close friends in places like Fiji ... At one point I was thinking of living a very different life, in the ministry, I saw myself there, working in churches in the Pacific.[79]

Morrison worked on developing a personal rapport with leaders James Marape, Frank Bainimarama and Manasseh Sogavare. He took Bainimarama and others to his church. His political aim was to build relations with the Pacific at the top and create a whole-of-government strategy. The Office of the Pacific was created in DFAT in 2019 to manage bilateral ties and Pacific assistance worth $1.44 billion in 2020–21. Its task is to coordinate the Pacific Step-up across all departments, with Foreign Minister Payne providing the NSC with a progress report every six months.

Morrison wants to be the prime minister of the Pacific. This priority is driven by deep strategic intent. The Pacific is Australia's metropolitan zone but its states are fragile, with China keen to penetrate using credit, chasing a naval facility and working to outflank Australia. Successive governments have failed to show the Pacific the priority it warrants. This began to change under Turnbull as Prime Minister and Bishop as Foreign Minister with the launch of the Pacific Step-up policy.

At the start of the 2019 election year, Morrison visited Fiji and Vanuatu, an unusual move for a prime minister outside Pacific Islands Forum meetings. The year before, Australia and Fiji had announced the redevelopment of the Black Rock military base as a regional hub for police and peacekeeping training, deflecting moves by Beijing. Australia is partnering with Papua New Guinea (PNG) to redevelop the Lombrum naval base, located on Manus Island and situated strategically on the northern approach to the PNG mainland. The facility, under PNG ownership, will enhance its naval capability and serve as a base for Australian and US vessels in the Southwest Pacific.

Later in 2019, Morrison and Bainimarama exchanged reciprocal visits and signed the 'Vuvale partnership' that underwrites closer economic and security ties. In August 2020, Morrison and Marape signed the PNG–Australia Comprehensive Strategic and Economic Partnership (CSEP), elevating the relationship around core principles including a pledge to establish a Bilateral Security Treaty and extend military cooperation and interoperability. Australia expanded its diplomatic footprint so that it was represented in every Pacific Islands Forum country. The response to COVID-19 saw a shift in health and social priorities with Morrison pledging 15 million vaccine doses to the Pacific by mid-2022, the aim being full vaccination.

Dave Sharma says of Morrison:

I don't think any prime minister in my profes-sional memory has shown this sort of personal commitment to the Pacific. Morrison has led this himself. He spends time in contact with the leaders of Papua New Guinea, Fiji and Solomon Islands and I am always surprised about the detail he has about what's happening in the Pacific. He understands Pacific leaders put a lot on the personal respect shown to them.[80]

The Pacific Step-up is driven by Morrison's personal commitment to improve conditions in the region and limit China's strategic penetration. Australia's message to the region is manifest: it expects to remain the 'partner of choice' for the Pacific. In turn, Pacific leaders understand that if China is permitted to establish strategic facilities there, it would have an impact not just on the Pacific Islands region, but on Australia.

After his 2019 election victory, Morrison appointed his close colleague Alex Hawke as minister for International Development and the Pacific. The first country Morrison visited after the election victory was Solomon Islands, taking Hawke with him, again signalling his priorities.

'I always thought it was his number one foreign policy priority,' Hawke said. 'For me, the Step-up would evolve to be the leading policy of the region. The PM's mission was to ensure that Defence and Foreign Affairs were cooperating, so we had the development dollars and the military's great involvement. We support the sovereignty of these countries and we oppose anybody's efforts to undermine sovereignty.'[81]

The Pacific Step-up strategy has three pillars: supporting economies, people-to-people ties and security priorities. For Morrison, the key is follow-through. Having an NSC focus on the Pacific and lifting the tempo of ministerial visits have been essential. The security factor is pervasive. In 2017, Turnbull and Bishop moved with urgency when Solomon Islands decided to team with Huawei to build an undersea fibre-optic cable from Honiara to Sydney, with Australian security agencies warning against it in the strongest possible terms. The upshot was an Australian government–funded cable network linking Honiara, Port Moresby and Sydney.

'China is everywhere in the Pacific now and that's been the change in recent years,' Hawke says.

We've always said if China wanted to fund schools or hospitals or help people improve their lives, we'd be supportive. But we question countries when they come in for their own motivation. The Prime Minister was concerned about the changes that had come across the Pacific. He felt they weren't in its best interests and Australia had an important Step-up function.[82]

The Lowy Institute *Pacific Aid Map* annual update for 2021, however, suggests China's aid may have peaked in 2018. Chinese aid to the Pacific fell by 31 per cent from US$246 million in 2018 to US$169 million in 2019.[83]

The biggest point of tension with Pacific Islands countries is climate change, and this came to a head at the August 2019 Pacific Islands Forum meeting in Tuvalu when Pacific leaders demanded that Morrison go beyond the Paris Agreement and take an explicit stand against coal. For Pacific leaders, climate change is an existential threat. They leveraged this into international prominence. Within the United Nations process, they had standing as the states most vulnerable to rising sea levels. Jacinda Ardern joined the public pile-on against Morrison.

Morrison and the Australian delegation worked furiously to outline Australia's action on emissions and its financial support to the region on climate, but also warned that Australia would not compromise its economic sovereignty. In the end, Morrison got a communiqué that avoided Australia's 'red lines'. But the respite was temporary. Australia and the Pacific remain divided by competing interests over climate change. The tensions between them will only get worse, and it is difficult to see how Morrison can quarantine climate change from the broader relationship.

Senior DFAT officials privately worried at the outset that Morrison's Pacific focus might mean a shrinking foreign policy. By 2020, however, the opposing story had materialised. As the COVID-19 pandemic kept heads of government confined to their offices, a new brand of global diplomacy unfolded with Morrison in a conspicuous role.

'For Australia, COVID levelled the diplomatic playing field,' a senior official said.

> The Prime Minister can conduct diplomacy from his office, not fly for 10 or 20 hours to have a meeting. This brought Morrison further and faster up the diplomatic learning curve than anyone could have imagined. In this sense, his first three years in office were the equivalent of John Howard's first six years in terms of hard diplomatic experience.

During 2020, Morrison got an appetite for head-of-government diplomacy and had an effective message: Australia's success at managing the pandemic. That message lost much of its traction during 2021, but initially Morrison sold Australia's success as evidence of all-round resilience and governing competence. The pandemic matured Morrison as a foreign policy leader. The leader who bemoaned 'negative globalism' in his 2019 Lowy Lecture, while justifiably concerned about the performance and behaviour of some multilateral institutions, had by 2020 turned into an advocate for improving the multilateral rules-based order. In a sense, he had been mugged by reality.

Morrison's 2019 remarks revealed an equivocation and suspicion about globalisation that constituted a departure from established Australian foreign policy. The context was Trump's 'Fortress America' revolt and growing alarm among conservative voters in Western nations, including Australia, about multilateral decisions infringing on national sovereignty. Morrison had warned against 'a negative globalism that coercively seeks to impose a mandate from an often ill-defined borderless global community'.[84] This exposed a strong sentiment, not spelt out, but primarily assumed to refer to pressure on Australia to improve its climate change targets, which Morrison saw as conflicting with the mandate he had won at the election. He was disputing the legitimacy of international pressure that sought policy changes from Australia at odds with the outcome of its democratic process.

However, Morrison cast his net far wider. He paraphrased the Howard dictum from 2001 saying that in conducting Australia's international engagements, 'we will decide our interests and the circumstances in which we seek to pursue them'. This was an assertion of national sovereignty against international norms. Morrison asked DFAT to conduct a 'comprehensive audit' of global institutions and processes where Australia had important stakes. This was supported by the conservative wing of the Liberal Party. It created the potential for wider policy changes putting limits on Australia's international aspirations.

This venture, however, was plagued by a contradiction inherent in Morrison's speech. He said Australia had no interest in isolationism or protectionism. The purpose was to ensure a greater Australian involvement in 'setting global standards', which implied deeper international and multilateral involvement.[85]

In the end, no significant policy revisions flowed from the DFAT review. The language of 'negative globalism' disappeared. Morrison's pragmatism prevailed against his earlier ideological stance. It would be wrong, however, to conclude that Morrison had changed his mind on the principle of democratic sovereignty. He believed multilateral institutions obtained their ultimate legitimacy from the participation of nation states.

In Morrison's view, the critical factor was changing events and circumstances. In response to trade retaliation from China, its defiance of international norms, and a global pandemic, Morrison became more a supporter of global institutions than a critic. COVID-19 was a shared crisis and Morrison, with conspicuous help from Foreign Minister Payne, supported a stronger, more independent and transparent World Health Organization (WHO) – the lesson being that the 'international order is as important as ever'.[86] Morrison talked of 'positive globalism', looked to the World Trade Organization (WTO) to check China's tactics and sought to ensure global institutions were fit for purpose and accountable to member states.

During 2020, the year of virtual diplomacy, the intensity of Morrison's engagement with foreign leaders was probably unmatched in our history. Records from the Prime Minister's office show that Morrison made one overseas trip to Japan, conducted 55 virtual discussions with other leaders and participated in 20 virtual summits that included multilateral as well as bilateral meetings. Morrison says in total he had 122 phone calls with foreign leaders. While COVID-19 domestic decision-making reached a frantic pace, Morrison was engaged on a weekly basis in extensive head-of-government diplomacy that ranged from Afghanistan to Vietnam.[87]

'You'd have to go back to Curtin for the pace and intensity of it,' Morrison told the author.[88] The most calls were made, unsurprisingly, to New Zealand's Ardern, but there were multiple calls with the leaders of PNG, Japan, Indonesia, the United States, the United Kingdom and India. In addition, there were text messages and letters. While Morrison's activism focused on the Indo-Pacific, the list of European leaders was also long.

Morrison in 2020 became comfortable with – and almost compulsive about – head-of-government dialogue. The dividends were many and varied, one of the most obvious being the September 2021 agreement with British Prime Minister Boris Johnson on a 4 million Pfizer vaccine dose swap, Australia getting its supply up-front in September to assist the country's immediate needs and returning the favour to the United Kingdom during its winter. This testified to Morrison's investment in Johnson, a relationship between two very different conservative leaders.

Payne was engaged in her own brand of 'virtual' diplomacy. Asked to nominate her main contribution as foreign minister, she said, 'building relationships and strengthening partnership networks'.[89]

Activism cannot be equated with results, but it does lead to results. Three years into the job, Morrison had travelled a long way – from amateur to activist. But it is the quality of activism that matters, and China became his test.

CHAPTER FIVE

Morrison's China challenge

The China story became the dominant theme in Scott Morrison's foreign policy. That was Beijing's choice, but it also reflected Morrison's character: he would push back when provoked. The decline in Australia–China relations betrayed a cultural mistrust superimposed on a deepening strategic tension. As provocation was matched by provocation, neither Beijing nor Canberra had the will to halt the decline.

The revolution in China policy occurred under Malcolm Turnbull, but Morrison, a participant in that project, embraced his inheritance. When Morrison became Prime Minister in August 2018, Australia's relations with China were already in serious decline. Beijing had limited ministerial visits and was moving against some Australian exports.

As China's punitive actions grew, Morrison's instinctual response was to push back and present the China tensions in terms of Australian values and sovereignty.

But pushback was linked to patience. Morrison sought, in speech after speech, to keep the door open. 'We are committed to deepening our comprehensive strategic partnership with China,' he said in his first foreign policy speech as Prime Minister.[90] He wanted to limit the damage. In August 2020, he still said his approach was 'strategic patience and consistency', and that it was in Beijing's interest to recognise the relationship was 'mutually beneficial'.[91]

Over time, such appeals became hollow rituals. Morrison made no policy concessions to Beijing and saw no valid ground for concessions, a view shared by most of his advisers. The assumption on which Morrison and his government operated was that the Australian decisions that provoked China were national interest imperatives and responses to China's high-tech intrusions, monolithic state power and economic coercion. Australia was not for turning.

Patience was also emblematic of a diplomatic void. Given Beijing's eventual freeze on ministerial dialogue and Australia's determination to stand by its policy decisions, the scope for diplomacy was extremely limited. Morrison's approach was to stand his ground, signal a willingness to re-engage and try to avoid gratuitous offence, although many Coalition parliamentarians indulged in strident criticism of China with the Prime Minister's office far too slow to impose discipline.

As 2020 advanced and China's intimidation intensified, Morrison's mood hardened. The extent of China's trade retaliation against Australia and the release of a series of political demands had a profound impact on the Morrison government and its advisers. China's behaviour left the indelible impression it was a coercive power, not to be trusted; any back-down by Australia became completely untenable.

The more pressure China applied, the more determined Morrison became that Australia must not buckle. Morrison saw it as a test of national willpower and of Australia's sovereign authority. There was also an inevitable personal element – Morrison felt China was trying to intimidate and break him as Prime Minister.

Former ambassador to China Geoff Raby said the combination of pushback and patience meant the relationship descended to its 'lowest point' since diplomatic relations had begun. Australia's once 'almost unrivalled access' to China's leadership was now replaced with the absence of official contact. Neither side would pay the price to heal the rift.[92]

The consequence for Australia was that bilateral relations became hostage to the extent of Beijing's displeasure. In 2021, President Biden's Indo-Pacific coordinator Kurt Campbell advised Australia to settle in 'for the long haul' against a China that seemed to be 'unyielding', a view Morrison had long since reached.

Informal high-level discussions between DFAT and its Chinese counterparts revealed the depth of China's aggravation. Beijing blamed Australia for the breakdown. It conceded nothing and admitted no mistakes. 'They are determined to bring us to heel,' was the advice given to Morrison.

In her farewell address to the National Press Club, outgoing DFAT secretary and former ambassador to China Frances Adamson said:

China speaks of a 'new type of international relations' as if it is a fairer way, an improvement. But underneath it is the same old power politics, the raw assertion of national interests . . . Insecurity and power can be a volatile combination . . . It means, among other things, that China is undergoing a steep loss of influence in Australia and many other countries.[93]

The deterioration in relations had reached a significant stage under Turnbull. Beijing's coolness on ministerial dealings with Australia was highlighted when no Australian ministers were invited to the April 2018 Boao Forum, known as the Asian Davos, in China.[94] At that time, Foreign Minister Bishop had not visited China for more than two years. Turnbull's last visit had been to attend the G20 summit in September 2016.

The foreign interference laws and their presentation by Turnbull in late 2017 were factors in China's hostility. Campaigning in the Bennelong by-election and referring to Chairman Mao's 1949 declaration that 'the Chinese people have stood up', Turnbull declared: 'The Australian people stand up.' He was stung by the criticism this provoked. 'I was surprised by the ferocity of the reaction to the foreign interference legislation,' Turnbull said. 'It was so over the top even to the point of accusing me of being a racist.' He said that claiming offence because he quoted Mao was 'unhinged'.[95]

At the same time, there were warnings and disruption on the trade front concerning foreign students, beef, wine and coal.[96] Trade Minister Simon Birmingham, while not absolving China, was restrained in most of his public comments. Turnbull had played down the trade interruptions but identified another issue: 'panic in the Australian business community'.[97]

But Turnbull knew he had a China problem and he sought to fix it. Turnbull wrote to Xi Jinping on 22 May and got Bishop to deliver the letter personally to her Chinese counterpart, Wang Yi. Turnbull sought to explain his 'Australian people stand up' remark, saying it was intended to convey respect. In August 2018, Turnbull delivered what he later called a 'reconciliation' speech in Sydney, where he spoke positively about the China relationship. But there was little evidence Beijing was interested in reconciliation.[98]

Morrison inherited a fractured relationship, yet communications had not terminated. Foreign Minister Payne visited Beijing in November 2018, where she met Foreign Minister Wang Yi. Later, she held a phone conversation with him and in September 2019 they had a 30-minute meeting when they were in New York for the UN General Assembly. That was their last meeting in person. Their last phone discussion was in February 2020 in the context of COVID-19. They have not spoken since. Payne has written letters but received no reply.

Under Morrison, the deterioration became more entrenched. By the second half of 2020, Morrison saw the clash as involving a bigger question: would Australia have the resilience to avoid succumbing to the status of Chinese client state?

Once Morrison embraced this framing, every aspect of China policy assumed new meaning. For the Prime Minister, this was about foreign policy, but also an existential challenge: the ultimate issue was Australia's autonomy as a liberal democracy. Within the Morrison government, senior advisers saw the issue as having international significance around this test: was Australia a nation able to confront China's bullying, or an example of how not to manage ties with Beijing?

One senior official said, 'Australia is on the leading edge of a global struggle over how the rise of China will play out.' It was not about China being a direct military threat to Australia, and ministers made no suggestions to this effect. It was, rather, about China's penchant for using coercive power against Australia to extract changes in foreign and domestic policy.

After leaving office, Turnbull spoke more openly about the task Australia faced, using terms he would never have used as Prime Minister, yet sentiments Morrison would probably share. In May 2021, drawing upon a famous Cold War analogy, Turnbull said, 'We do not want to be to China what Finland was to the Soviet Union. That's the bottom line.'[99] The reference to 'Finlandisation' – the term used to describe Finland's accommodation of the

Soviet Union during the Cold War – offered an insight into government thinking.

The conclusion Morrison reached, conveyed to a senior minister, was that China 'would push as far as the rest of the world allows it' and if Australia 'does not stand its ground here, we will be forced to stand on more difficult and weaker ground later on'.

While some commentators lamented Australia's inept diplomacy with China and its inability to improve relations, Morrison's priority lay elsewhere: building across-the-board resilience against China's intimidation.

Andrew Shearer, appointed Director-General of the Office of National Intelligence (ONI) in December 2020 after being cabinet secretary, had Morrison's confidence and argued for a dual approach to China based on resilience: protecting domestic institutions and promoting an international alignment to balance Beijing. The bulk of foreign and security thinking within government was broadly in line with Morrison's approach. Dissenters were few on the ground. Australian policymaking from the 2003 Iraq war onwards reveals that once a prime minister takes a firm position, there is little appetite for internal questioning by officials within the system.

Building upon his thesis in the 2017 Foreign Policy White Paper, Richard Maude says, 'Beijing wants the Australia–China relationship to work only on terms it sets: access to its market in return for silence on issues like human rights and cyberattacks, compliance with China's "core interests" such as the South China Sea and Taiwan, and accommodation of China's tech companies.'[100] In an unmistakable reference to China, Frances Adamson said in 2020, 'If Australia did not have an agenda and exercise agency, then we would have simply to accept the terms dictated by others.'[101] Her predecessor Peter Varghese told the author, 'China does not want to impose its ideology on Australia. It wants Australia to defer to its core interests [but] Australia does not want to see a return to the Middle Kingdom because we have no interest in being a tributary state.'[102]

Context is everything in explaining Morrison's policy. He became Prime Minister at a time when both Australia and the United States had made fresh announcements that amplified their distrust of China. Australia banned Huawei because it would not trust a Chinese company in its critical infrastructure, while US Vice President Mike Pence delivered, in effect, the epitaph of America's engagement with China in his speech to the Hudson Institute. Closing an era and resetting the relationship, Pence said the 'hope' that China engagement had offered since 1972 'has gone unfulfilled'.[103]

Constraining China in its assault on Australia and its regional destabilisation became the central organising principle of Morrison's foreign policy. It touched everything. His aim was to leverage Australia's economic, diplomatic, military and political influence with allies and neighbours. While keen to see a thaw in relations with China, Morrison recognised that China's assertive behaviour demanded not just a bilateral but a regional and global response.

'Accelerating trends are working against our interests,' he said. Australia's task was to build 'on the strong cooperation with the United States, Japan and India, stepping up in the Pacific, supporting Southeast Asia and engaging ASEAN as a steadfast partner'. In June 2021, en route to the G7 meeting of democracies in Cornwall, Morrison said the defining issue was 'escalating great power competition' and that Australia's national interest was 'inextricably linked to an open, inclusive and resilient Indo-Pacific region'.

Morrison identified two goals for the region: a 'strategic balance', obviously against China; and a balance that 'favours freedom' and 'liberal democracy', signalling that the contest with China went to values that were non-negotiable. Morrison said it was vital for 'liberal democracies and advanced economies' to 'align their thinking', whether on COVID-19, economic recovery, national security or strengthening multilateral institutions.[104]

This vision of the China problem transcended the repair of bilateral ties. Adamson said of Beijing–Canberra relations:

> It won't be a reset . . . This will take a very long time because it's not just about Australia. It's about a growing list of countries that are discovering if they seek to act in their own interests, in ways which China sees are contrary to its, China will seek to exert pressure.[105]

Critics told Morrison he must display more skilful and nuanced diplomacy in dealing with China. But the reaction in government was dismissive. 'A good op-ed piece doesn't translate into viable foreign policy' was one adviser's reaction. With every trade retaliation, with each 'wolf warrior' attack on Australia from Beijing, Morrison felt vindicated in his judgment, and the cycle was self-reinforcing. Beijing was convincing Morrison that his hard line was the only response.

Morrison's China journey from 2018 to 2021 was a wild ride. Along the way, there were road bumps, improvisations and diplomatic mistakes, but long-run strategic intent.

It had begun after Morrison's 2018 ascension to the prime ministership when he initially clung to the Howard Doctrine. In the region for his first round of summitry amid growing US–China tensions, Morrison said, 'Australia doesn't have to choose and we won't choose.' Australia would navigate its way, working 'constructively' with both the United States and China.[106]

Meeting Chinese Premier Li Keqiang on the sidelines of the joint ASEAN–East Asia Summit events in Singapore in November 2018, Morrison said there would be periodic difficulties, but a mature relationship should be able to cope. Li told Morrison this could be a 'turning point' after 'ups and downs' in relations. After the meeting, Morrison said Australia would work with China across the 'broad-based relationship'.[107]

Yet there would be no business as usual. Australia was engaged in a decisive shift from the Howard formula that had worked so well in its time.

Morrison accepted the view of China that Turnbull was able to express after he left office: 'We recognised that China's goal was to supplant the United States as the leading power in the region and that was plainly not in our interests.'[108] There is little doubt that Morrison's ultimate goal is to deny China regional strategic primacy because that is seen as a serious blow to Australia's interests and autonomy.

This is an unprecedented policy ambition, unique in Australia's history and not necessarily achievable. Morrison's strategy is multidimensional: it aims to deepen the alliance and military partnership with the United States, boost Australia's defence budget and capability to project power into the region, and promote new ties with Indo-Pacific countries to build a deeper sense of common purpose.

Resilience against China is a factor in everything Morrison does: the Pacific Step-up; development of the Lombrum naval base on Manus Island with PNG leader Peter O'Neill; his warnings to Pacific nations against the trap of loans from China; his immediate bonding with Japan's Prime Minister Abe in Darwin in November 2018 where they pledged 'deeper defence cooperation' (the sincerity of Morrison's dealings with Abe contrasted with the hollowness of his dealings with China)[109]; and the development of the Quad with the United States, Japan and India.

Morrison has a quick grasp of power realities. An observer of prime ministers, Peter Varghese calls Morrison an 'instinctual politician' rather than a 'conceptual thinker'.[110] But Morrison did not become Prime Minister after just 11 years in parliament without a strong streak of self-belief and boldness. He acted upon his judgment.

Australia's former ambassador to Beijing Geoff Raby warns that Australia is making a fateful blunder. 'China neither threatens Australia militarily nor its values,' Raby says. He says China is plagued by anxieties and vulnerabilities that 'all but rule out the projection of power by military means beyond its near abroad' and that China is 'unlikely to become a regional hegemon'. For Raby, Australia is misinterpreting the China threat and making a related mistake – it is acting on the assumption of China as a strategic competitor. This is 'now ingrained in Canberra's worldview' and is bringing Australia into dangerous alignment with the United States, a superpower rival to China whose interests do not always coincide with those of Australia.[111]

But another former ambassador and later Liberal MP Dave Sharma argues that Morrison's China policy is world leading:

I think Morrison has been at the leading edge of the global debate about China. He has been one of the first leaders to recognise and articulate the view that China's external policy has fundamentally changed. We were one of the first countries to experience this and Morrison was one of the first leaders to call it out. I think he has helped to shift global opinion, particularly among the G20 nations. Increasingly, these nations are now seeing China as a strategic actor and a challenge to the post–Second World War order.[112]

There were two shadows over Morrison's strategy: the unreliability of Trump's America, given the president's disdain for allies, and uncertainty about Indo-Pacific solidarity and resolution. But such doubts did not deflect from the core strategy. China's bullying threatened the national interest and it rubbed the Australian character up the wrong way.

Morrison kept his nerve in the face of Trump's unpredictability. Trump initiated a dangerous trade war with China from which there would be no real winners, culminating in the United States placing tariffs of US\$550 billion on Chinese imports and Beijing retaliating with US\$185 billion on US imports. Then, in January 2020, came a heavily qualified respite in the form of a trade deal that undid some of the tariffs. Amid this assault on the global trade system, Morrison stayed on safe ground, warning against rising trade protectionism and working to salvage the WTO against Trump's offensive.[113]

But the Trump–Xi dispute transcended trade. Trump wanted to smash the momentum driving China's rising economic power. It was a struggle between rival ideological systems. Trump's fantasy was to pressure Xi into a grand bargain on US terms while the two leaders engaged in nauseating declarations of mutual praise.[114] Neither a US–China economic conflict nor an ideological conflict was in Australia's interests.

Trump had cancelled the convergence principle that long underpinned US policy towards China. This was the belief expounded by President George H. W. Bush after the 1989 Tiananmen Square massacre that commercial developments meant 'the move to democracy becomes inexorable'. In his speech to the Hudson Institute, Vice President Pence buried this doctrine as a misguided fantasy. 'We assumed that a free China was inevitable,' Pence said. But Beijing instead had set its sights on 'controlling 90 per cent of the world's most advanced industries' and was seeking 'to push the US from the Western Pacific'. Pence said a 'new consensus' was rising in the United States against Beijing's predatory behaviour with the upshot that 'America's commitment to the Indo-Pacific has never been stronger'.[115] The validity of this claim remains to be tested.

The immense domestic authority Morrison felt after his 2019 election victory quickly translated into foreign policy, yet the gulf between his optimistic rhetoric and his strategic realism was widening. After the election, Morrison said he saw Australia–China relations as 'improving'. Australia's policies towards China left 'large scope for cooperation' and he repudiated the 'false framework' of Australia having to choose between America and China. 'My government is going to be very positive in rejecting that dynamic,' he said. Morrison played down any talk of regional conflict.[116]

He still talked up the comprehensive strategic partnership with China, saying that sometimes 'hard calls' were necessary in the national interest and both countries would make them. China's economic success, he said, 'is good for China, it is good for Australia'. Noting the huge infrastructure needs of the region, Morrison said, Australia 'welcomes the contribution that the Belt and Road Initiative can make', referring to President Xi Jinping's globally ambitious infrastructure promotion scheme that is also an instrument of economic and strategic influence. He insisted Australia had no interest in 'economic' containment of China. On political relations, Morrison said, 'While we will be clear-eyed that our political differences will affect aspects of our engagement, we are determined that our relationship not be dominated by areas of disagreement.'[117]

This was a public view of China far more optimistic than that of the United States. Claims that the two nations had identical views on China were wrong. Morrison kept the door open in case China changed its mind. Most of the time his language about China was prudent. 'Morrison has made clear he wants dialogue and a respectful relationship with Beijing, while at the same time he has presided over a shift in our China policy and also a shift in the global debate,' Sharma said.[118] To the extent that Beijing's trade retaliation against Australia continued, Morrison's intent was to ensure Beijing was blamed.

Yet the strategic challenge Morrison depicted was increasingly dire. He warned the global rules-based order was under threat and the rise in US–China rivalry exposed the region to a 'new threshold' of risk. Morrison's focus was on changes to the regional order to accommodate China's rise while preserving the peace. However, he saw in Beijing's tactics that 'economic coercion is increasingly employed as a tool of statecraft'.[119]

Morrison's response to China had both domestic and external dimensions. The security services had only reinforced their warnings from 2017. Former ASIO head Duncan Lewis told the author:

> Australia is on China's radar; we are big enough to matter to the Chinese, but we are small enough to push around. We need to be very careful we don't let our security guard down to a point where we wake up on a certain morning and find that our political and societal institutions have lost their independence of decision-making.[120]

On retirement in late 2019, Lewis was replaced by Mike Burgess, a decision driven by Home Affairs Minister Peter Dutton. ASIO assessed that China's activities threatened Australia's security and vacuumed up intellectual property via cyber theft. ASIO advice was almost never contradicted by policy departments.

By 2020, Morrison had reached a series of relentless conclusions about China. First, that President Xi was committed to a new phase of strategic assertion fuelled by Chinese nationalism. Second, that the Australian security decisions to which China had objected were justified. Third, that Australia had more to lose than gain by submitting to Beijing's intimidation. Fourth, that the need to strike a new balance of power against China meant Australia had to look to the United States as the linchpin. And fifth, that Australia must be proactive in building coalitions of interest across the Indo-Pacific and Southeast Asia to encourage regional solidarity.

This was the backdrop to the most decisive event of Morrison's leadership: the global pandemic. COVID-19 ripped across the world, claiming millions of lives, forcing governments into emergency measures, precipitating a global recession and accentuating tensions between China and the West. The pandemic would also accentuate the government's conclusions about China.

In December 2019, there were signs that an atypical pneumonia was spreading among residents in Wuhan, the capital of Hubei province in China. Doctors inside the country who raised the alarm were intimidated into silence. On 1 January 2020, the Huanan Seafood Wholesale Market in Wuhan was shut down. On 7 January, Xi Jinping and members of the country's Politburo Standing Committee discussed the outbreak. On 14 January, the WHO said there had been 'limited' human-to-human transmission of a coronavirus, though it later revealed Beijing concealed much of the story. On 30 January, WHO Director-General Tedros Adhanom Ghebreyesus declared a Public Health Emergency of International

Concern – a belated decision given the virus had by then been identified in 18 countries. After returning from China, the Director-General said China had set 'a new standard for outbreak response'. Subsequent investigations raised unresolved questions about the origins of the virus – whether from the wet market or from a laboratory in Wuhan.

Australia had moved quickly, acting on advice from Chief Medical Officer Brendan Murphy and Health Minister Greg Hunt. Murphy exercised his power under the Biosecurity Act and declared, in effect, a pandemic threat. On 1 February, the government imposed a travel ban on China, a decision criticised by Beijing and the WHO.

Deputy head of mission at China's Canberra embassy Wang Xining said, 'We are not happy about the situation because we were not alerted.' The *Global Times* newspaper said Australia was 'betraying its characteristically blind and senseless shadowing of US policies and practices with regard to China'. The WHO Director-General opposed travel bans on China, saying they could cause 'fear and stigma'. China invoked the WHO in its criticism of Australia.[121]

The Morrison government was under public attack from Beijing for protecting Australian lives. Canberra concluded that the WHO's stance was a dereliction of its mandate.

Australia's response to the health crisis was conducted through the NSC. From February to April 2020, the government's preoccupation was the COVID-19 challenge, domestic responses and the global threat posed by the pandemic. Marise Payne said, 'you cannot over-emphasise' the role of the NSC in COVID decision-making.[122] NSC ministers were alarmed at the extent of China's cover-up and how the concealed origins of the virus had allowed the global explosion. The WHO's leadership was heavily influenced by China and did not declare the crisis a pandemic until 11 March, a fortnight after Australia.

In April, President Trump announced that America would halt its funding of the WHO despite the crisis. 'I sympathise with his criticisms and I've made a few of my own,' Morrison said. 'We called this thing weeks before the WHO did.' But Australia did not follow Trump's decision.[123]

Morrison's frustration boiled over when the WHO supported the re-opening of China's wet markets. 'It's unfathomable, frankly,' the Prime Minister said. Politicians from both sides attacked the decision. Hunt said that if Australia had not acted on 1 February but had followed WHO advice, then 'the virus would have ripped through the Australian community and led to massive human losses'.[124] Director of Epidemiology at the Doherty Institute and a co-opted member of the panel advising the national cabinet, Jodie McVernon said, 'We have averted a catastrophe. You only have to look at New York, London and Spain.'[125]

A senior official told the author, 'When the PM said this was a fight on two fronts – health and the economy – there was always a third front in our minds: China.'

China's COVID-19 behaviour reinforced earlier messages from the intelligence agencies that Beijing was untrustworthy. Ministers felt that this time the world had paid a high price. Morrison refused to endorse the theory taken up by Trump that the virus may have originated from a Wuhan lab. But Trump contributed to the atmospherics. With his health response failing, Trump branded COVID-19 the 'Chinese virus' and accused Beijing of a cover-up.

During months of NSC debate, ministers focused on the dual failures of China and the WHO. Home Affairs Minister Dutton said on 17 April that with more than 60 coronavirus deaths nationwide, people in Australia wanted 'answers and transparency' from China. He said the Australian people had a right to know. 'It would certainly be demanded of us if Australia was at the epicentre of this virus making its way into society,' Dutton said. 'I do think there will be a reset about the way in which the world interacts with China.'[126] It was a revealing sentiment. Deputy Prime Minister Michael McCormack said China had questions to answer, and senior ministers felt China should be held to account. There was also another sentiment, that if Australia did not openly discuss China's accountability, it would be succumbing to Beijing's pressure.

During talks among a small group of senior ministers, the idea of an inquiry into the origins of the virus was raised. The inquiry question was also raised in the NSC, but there was no formal submission and no extensive assessment undertaken by DFAT. The inquiry idea gained its logic from the view that the failures of China and the WHO should be addressed and corrective mechanisms identified. An inquiry was seen as sound and safe domestic politics, too.

Morrison was emboldened by Australia's success in fighting the virus. The Prime Minister's office and Payne's office were talking about calling for an inquiry. But there had been no government decision when Payne called for an international inquiry on the ABC *Insiders* program on 19 April. Formal approval for such an initiative had not been given by either the NSC or federal cabinet. It came as a surprise to most ministers. Frances Adamson, as head of DFAT, had no prior knowledge of her minister's statement.

There is only one conclusion: the proposal was driven by politics, not diplomacy. Morrison and Payne wanted Australia to take a stand. An inquiry was a logical step, but the Morrison government had acted before it had consulted.

Payne's remarks were measured, but their content was explosive. She said the key issue was 'transparency from China'. From the outset, Payne targeted China and, to a lesser extent, the WHO. She said it was 'fundamental' to get 'an independent review mechanism' to examine 'the genesis of the virus', along with 'the openness with which information was shared' with the WHO and other world leaders. Payne said the WHO could not conduct the inquiry since it mixed 'poacher and gamekeeper'. Reinforcing Dutton's remarks, she said that she expected the virus meant relationships between Australia and China 'will be changed in some ways', but described the China relationship as 'well founded'.[127]

This was a big step – an Australian initiative on a global scale. It was not done under pressure from or at the request of the United States. The Labor Party supported the government, with shadow health spokesman Chris Bowen saying China should cooperate with the inquiry.

The Chinese Foreign Ministry criticised Payne, saying Beijing was 'firmly opposed' to the proposal. Within days, China's ambassador to Australia, Cheng Jingye, denounced Morrison's campaign and refused to accept that the virus had originated in a Wuhan wet market. He accused Australia of being 'politically motivated' and acting at Washington's behest. He warned that the Chinese public was 'frustrated, dismayed and disappointed', and Australia was risking economic repercussions. He suggested ordinary people would say, 'Why should we drink Australian wine? Eat Australian beef?'[128]

China's state media went on the offensive. The *Global Times* said, 'This is an all-out crusade against China and Chinese culture, led by Australia.' Morrison said the proposed inquiry was 'entirely reasonable and sensible'.[129] He said if the world had been alerted earlier, hundreds of thousands of lives might have been saved. He said the WHO should have powers similar to weapons inspectors to deal with future pandemics – an inflammatory and unrealistic suggestion.

The relationship had taken another blow. The question became: was it necessary for Australia to lead with the inquiry proposal? Any cost-benefit analysis would suggest the answer was no. Australia was under no pressure to take this lead. It was entirely voluntary. But Morrison never accepted this criticism and sought instead to rally international support for the proposal.

A balanced judgment is that Australia's inquiry call was justified on merit, yet damaging for China relations, possibly significantly. The decision-making process was inadequate. There is little evidence to suggest Australia assessed the depth of China's reaction. The Morrison government's move on the inquiry lacked the consideration the Turnbull government had given to the foreign interference laws and the Huawei decision.

Peter Varghese says, 'I think the way we pushed the COVID inquiry did us significant harm. China's management of the virus went to President Xi Jinping's authority and it clearly got under his skin. Our position may have been right, but it was not smart.'[130] Former Defence official and Bob Hawke adviser Hugh White says the government's mistake was to target China in its inquiry call. Without China's cooperation, the full story would never be exposed. 'Effective diplomacy is not about saying what you think is true,' White says. 'It is about saying what you need to say – and not saying what you don't need to say – to get a result.'[131]

In the end, the World Health Assembly voted to establish an independent inquiry, with Australia supporting a resolution coming from the European Union. It fell far short of Australia's initial demand.

Defending her position the following year, Payne said:

> We are 18 months into a pandemic that has devastated the global economy, has killed over four million people and we still do not know how it originated. We made that call because we felt it was an important step for the world to take. We could have taken the other path, be timid, do nothing. But Australia makes its points and it stands up.[132]

'It was the right thing to do,' Morrison says.

> It was a values response from me. That's what it fundamentally was – an instinctive values response that the world should know how this thing started so we can prevent it from happening again. We were experiencing a virus that was causing a global recession and taking millions of lives.[133]

The decision revealed a stubborn and more assertive Morrison, ready to lead. He felt this was an issue of both moral and international responsibility.

Beijing would have identified a common element running through Australia's initiatives from foreign interference laws, the Huawei ban and the virus inquiry push. Each had an impact beyond bilateral relations. They hurt China's global interests. Beijing repeated one of its propaganda lines: that Australia was operating on behalf of the United States against China's interests.

Turnbull later defended the government:

It is widely said that Morrison's and Payne's demand that there should be an independent inquiry into the origins of COVID was misguided or artless or ill-prepared. These criticisms are literally footnotes to footnotes. They are trivial. But the real point to that episode was the overreaction from Beijing. If Morrison and Payne's call for an independent inquiry had been met with no response, it would have sunk without trace ... What made it a story and an issue was the wild overreaction. And the sanctions, the trade sanctions, which followed, and which of course were building on ones previously imposed, only served to strengthen resolve in Australia and make public opinion more adverse to China than it was before.[134]

In May 2020, China's Ministry of Finance and Commerce ruled that Australia had subsidised and dumped barley, justifying a new 80.5 per cent tariff. Trade Minister Birmingham said he understood why people saw it as coercion. The same month, restrictions were applied to some Australian beef exports. China also moved against coal exports and in November 2020 imposed steep tariffs on Australian wine, claiming it was being dumped – an action that provoked the strongest response so far from Birmingham, who branded Beijing's claims a 'falsehood' and 'completely incompatible' with its WTO obligations. By the end of 2020, industries suffering from China's restrictions or threats included barley, wine, coal, education, beef, lamb, lobster, copper, timber, sugar and cotton.

Australia was not alone. But evidence suggested retaliation against Australia – when compared with Norway, South Korea and Canada – was more substantial.[135] Neither Birmingham nor his successor as Trade Minister Dan Tehan had any replies to their letters and calls to Beijing. In March 2021, Australia's ambassador Graham Fletcher, in a video briefing to business, called China's behaviour 'vindictive' and said, 'You've just got to imagine that, unexpectedly, you may lose your China market for no good reason other than that Beijing has decided to send a message to Canberra.'[136]

Yet the economic impact from China's retaliation was limited. A Lowy Institute analysis found that high commodity prices meant iron ore had delivered surging revenues and many exporters had shifted to new markets. Sales of coal, barley, copper, cotton, seafood and timber rose in other markets. Merchandise exports to China were worth $145 billion in 2020, just two per cent short of the peak in 2019.[137]

'Our economy has proven to be remarkably resilient,' Josh Frydenberg said after releasing a Treasury analysis. Specific industries and regions had been hurt, but the overall economic impact was 'relatively modest'. The Treasurer said Australian exports to China of the targeted goods accounted for just 5.9 per cent of total Australian exports. Many firms and industries had found new markets. Whether China would move against the big-ticket item of iron ore exports remained in the balance. Frydenberg's message was: Australia is coping, but there must be no complacency, and business has to build its resilience.[138]

By 2021, Morrison felt confident enough to say, 'Trade volumes with China are at their highest level. There is a co-dependence of our economies which is still real.' He made clear that defying Beijing's retaliation was a non-negotiable Australian stance. 'I don't underestimate there is cost here,' he said. 'There is a cost to maintaining the trajectory of our national character.' Asked if the public would continue to bear the cost, he replied, 'We must.'[139] Beijing's tactics had alienated public opinion while failing to break the government – a double defeat.

Much of the resetting of China policy since 2015 was based on the recognition that previous policies were untenable with a more assertive China. The process of reversing some of those old policies was politically dangerous. It was inevitable that Morrison's focus would fall on the Belt and Road Initiative (BRI). In a critical May 2017 meeting under the Turnbull government, the NSC assessed the BRI and decided against Australia signing up. The proposal under review would have linked Australia's Northern Development Program with the BRI.

This decision was taken on a mixture of financial and strategic grounds. The strong sentiment was that Australia would get no extra Chinese investment from signing. But this was reinforced by strategic concerns put in the meeting by then Defence Secretary Dennis Richardson, who said China pursued the BRI as a strategic lever and that Australia must be wary. The NSC decided Australia should consider Chinese investment decisions on a case-by-case basis and not ink a BRI agreement. In May 2019, Morrison said, 'We have a neutral position on that. We don't participate in it.'[140]

Yet the federal government failed to give firm advice to the Victorian Labor government in 2018 when the state briefly consulted with DFAT about signing up to the BRI. DFAT briefed the Andrews government, but gave no advice not to sign. That was a mistake. Morrison, not long Prime Minister when the Andrews government made its announcement, said, 'It hasn't been discussed with me, no. I mean, foreign policy is the domain of the Commonwealth government.'[141]

As China became more assertive, the Morrison government hardened its opposition to the BRI. 'We do not believe it is consistent with Australia's national interest,' Morrison said in June 2020. Facing domestic pressure over COVID-19 and state premiers flexing their powers in fighting the pandemic, Morrison and Payne announced in August 2020 an assertion of Commonwealth power – a new law enabling the foreign minister to review any existing and prospective arrangements between the states and foreign governments.

The aim was to veto Victoria's BRI agreement. Morrison now saw the agreement as contrary to the national interest. But the purpose was wider: to empower the national government to review all arrangements the states had entered into with foreign governments. But Australia's universities would be covered too, reflecting the view of intelligence agencies that they were a 'point of vulnerability'. Morrison said Australia must 'speak with one voice' in the world. The politics were a dream and Federal Labor endorsed the position.

The Morrison government's purpose was to change the mindset of state governments and institutions towards China. Senior ministers complained in private that the nation's leading institutions were reluctant to confront the security ramifications of dealing with China. The new law meant a range of agreements made with Chinese institutions would be reviewed, many in the university sector. The law gave the foreign minister the power to veto agreements, with the consequence of further antagonising China. Fundamental to the law's impact would be whether its primary purpose was to cancel existing agreements or serve as a disincentive or warning to institutions in pursuing new agreements. Initial signs are that Payne may exercise a degree of caution.[142]

Morrison's aim was to build Australia's resilience and reinforce his domestic profile of strength in the contest with Beijing. The conjunction between convenient domestic politics and China pushback was striking. The 2021 Lowy Institute Poll revealed a sharp decline in public approval of China, with 63 per cent saying it was more of a security threat than an economic partner; three years earlier, the figure was 12 per cent. The economic partner measure had fallen to 34 per cent compared with 82 per cent three years earlier.[143]

In November 2020, in an extraordinary display of ineptitude, the Chinese embassy in Canberra released to the media a dossier of 14 grievances, with an official saying that if Australia addressed these issues 'it would be conducive to a better atmosphere'. The demands took Beijing's resentment to a new high, an official commenting, 'China is angry. If you make China the enemy, China will be the enemy.'

This 'wolf warrior' dossier played into Morrison's hands. It made clear that China's economic retaliation was driven by political factors and most were demands on Australia that neither the government nor the public would concede. The complaints were about policies, presentation and democratic values. They went to foreign investment decisions, the Huawei ban, foreign interference laws, the COVID-19 inquiry, 'interference' in Xinjiang, Hong Kong and Taiwan, criticism over the South China Sea, vetoing Victoria's BRI agreement, actions against Chinese journalists in Australia, allegations about China's cyberattacks, criticism of the Communist Party by MPs and antagonistic media reports about China.[144]

During 2020, Morrison argued that China's campaign against Australia was an attack on the nation's values and identity. Now he had a document to prove his case. He said Australia's democracy and sovereignty 'are not up for trade. Australia will always be ourselves,' Morrison said. 'We will always set our own laws and our own rules according to our national interests – not at the behest of any other nation, whether that's the US or China or anyone else.'[145] It is easy to say Morrison exploited the 14 points for political purposes, but China offered Morrison a political gift that could hardly be ignored. Beijing further doomed its cause with the Australian public. Its misunderstanding of Australia was profound. Perhaps it didn't care.

The 14 points were 'unofficial' – a document given to media, not government. But they confirmed Morrison's strategic case against China. Raby lamented that it merely created 'greater hysteria' in the Australian media. In January 2021, confident public opinion was behind him, Morrison said he was happy to meet with President Xi Jinping, but only on a no-conditions basis.[146] In February 2021, Morrison was toughening up, saying China had changed since the comprehensive strategic partnership was formed and that 'we cannot pretend that things are as they were'.[147]

The domestic politics ran Morrison's way, but this was a trap – the temptation was to adopt a hard line knowing it would resonate with the public. As a senior minister, Peter Dutton developed a profile as the government's 'hard man' on China with tacit understanding that this suited the government's political interests. Turnbull now said of China, 'Allow them an elegant dismount.' Offering his verdict on China's tactics, Turnbull said, 'Has it resulted in Australia being more compliant? No, on the contrary, it's gone the other way.'[148]

Morrison's critics said he had no plan to deal constructively with the region's economic powerhouse. Morrison's answer, in effect, was to say his primary task was to deny China's intimidation of Australia.

Below the radar, the government searched for a settling point with China. It had considered a special envoy, but felt it was unviable. 'We have been very clear,' Payne said. 'We want to engage. Those offers have not been taken up.' She said the government was 'constantly' looking towards a point of stabilisation with China, but the public would never accept steps that 'compromised our sovereignty'.[149]

The government was sensitive to accusations that it deliberately sought a leadership role in taking a tough stand against China. Participants report the determining factor in NSC decisions was the perception of the Australian national interest, not seeking to lead for the sake of leading. 'We took the decisions on merit as they arose,' a senior official said. But Morrison and Payne were adamant: only strong leadership could check China's coercion. Payne said, 'If we don't exercise strong leadership in the region, then others will.'[150]

The core dispute is over the strategic direction on China. Geoff Raby said Australia has made the wrong call – its 'miscalculation' has been 'joining the US in competition with China'. Raby said Australia should have formally signed up to China's BRI, that our commitment to the Quad is a strategic mistake and our alignment with America only exposes Australia to the unpredictable tribulations America faces in dealing with China as a superpower rival.[151]

Linda Jakobson, founding director of the China Matters think tank, says:

I think Australia has managed its relations with China differently to other nations. This is the real reason Australia has been subjected to harsher treatment. Other nations when they acted, knowingly or unknowingly, in ways that displeased China have chosen quiet diplomacy, they haven't resorted to megaphone diplomacy and they haven't publicly chastised China. But Australia has openly chosen this course.[152]

Hugh White warns of Australia's limitations in seeking to decide the terms of the relationship with Beijing:

> Whether Australia likes it or not, it now faces hard choices whenever it wants to oppose China. As a sovereign state, Australia has the right to do as it wishes. But it must accept the consequences of its choices. No one likes to be pushed around, especially by a known bully, but power has its own logic that cannot be denied. So Australia needs to learn to pick its fights.[153]

That's right. The test, therefore, is which fights are essential to the national interest.

Many critics of Morrison's China policy actually support the policy decisions that offend China. Their critique goes to diplomacy – or the lack of it. Former ONA director-general Allan Gyngell says:

> In my view, most of the policy decisions have been entirely defensible whether you are talking about 5G or foreign interference legislation or the WHO inquiry. I believe where we have gone wrong is in

the implementation of those policies and in the diplomacy surrounding them. Policies that have been entirely defensible in terms of Australian sovereignty and national interest have too often been proclaimed and presented as Australia leading an international campaign against China and we're now reaping the consequences of that. I don't think those policy changes needed to produce the difficulties that we have seen.[154]

Linda Jakobson says the 'main problem' is the presentation – 'the way Australia has chosen to communicate, not the content of Australia's positions'.[155]

Peter Varghese favours the Morrison government, but concedes a lack of diplomacy. 'I believe the decisions Australian governments have taken on China were essentially right in substance,' he says. 'The decline in relations essentially arises from actions triggered by China. But sometimes our diplomacy surrounding those decisions was weak and counterproductive. A posture is not a policy.'[156]

Government advisers admit mistakes have been made in diplomacy and tone, including over-selling the 5G decision and ineptitude in the presentation of the virus inquiry. But they insist China's objection is to the content and substance of Australia's policy changes and no amount of diplomacy could have substituted for that. Richard Maude says, 'Some decisions could have been handled better. But the primary driver of Australia–China tensions is structural, the widening clash of interest and values.'[157]

The consequence is that in late 2021, Australia remains in the damaging situation of having no ministerial communication, let alone a working relationship, with the dominant power in East Asia, its major trading partner and the country destined to become the world's largest economy. The longer this continues, the more Australia's national interest will be impaired, with Morrison unable to address the defect.

Morrison's approach to China leaves the Howard Doctrine behind. While following Turnbull's path, his approach is different. Morrison is strong on conviction, but too often careless on diplomacy. His pushback against China fits too conveniently into domestic political needs. He instinctively grasps the power equation and seeks a new regional balance against China.

Alert to the clash of values, he sees China's coercion as a long-run existential danger to Australia's way of life and himself as a defender of Australia's values and identity. He believes Australia faces not a military threat, but a sovereignty threat. 'We want to be who we are,' he told the author. Morrison sees

Australia operating at the leading edge of China's coercion and he uses every possible forum to warn leaders to revise their outlooks and come to grips with China's new assertiveness. He judges that the China challenge constitutes a decisive moment in the nation's history that demands a resolute response based on national interests and national character. He feels as Prime Minister that China has sought to break his will, and he is determined this will never happen.

CHAPTER SIX

Managing Trump and Biden

More than any recent prime minister, Scott Morrison faced an exacting test of US alliance management, having to deal with two contrasting presidencies: the erratic unilateralism of the Republican Donald Trump and the progressive multilateralism of the Democrat Joe Biden.

The democracy that put Trump and then Biden into the White House reflected a nation traumatised by domestic divisions that cast doubt on the reliability of America's role in the world. Morrison, and Malcolm Turnbull before him, faced a more troubled America than any Australian leaders since the inauguration of the ANZUS Treaty in 1951.

The paradox facing Morrison was obvious: while Beijing's assertiveness created the need for Australia to align more closely with the United States, the reliability of the United States as a senior partner was coming under its most intense questioning in decades.

In managing Trump, Morrison followed the path walked by Turnbull. Morrison achieved a cordial personal relationship with Trump, but operated a defensive strategy, the aim being to avoid mishaps from Trump's idiosyncratic compulsions and scepticism about allies. Both prime ministers sought to befriend and humour Trump, but at the same time they 'worked' the administration, focusing on more reliable senior figures. Morrison established a personal connection with the Vice President and Secretary of State.

'I engaged him [Trump] personally,' Morrison said. 'But I didn't just engage him; the key to my relationship with the [Trump] administration was deeply rooted in my relationship with Mike Pence and Mike Pompeo.' He said his contact with Pompeo was 'weekly, not necessarily on the phone, but we were regular correspondents'. They had a faith connection. 'We're evangelical Christians,' Morrison said. And Pence called himself an evangelical Catholic.[158]

Richard Maude described the situation:

Both Turnbull and Morrison recognised that the narrow nationalism of Trump's 'America First' approach could damage Australia and that Trump was immune to facts or logic once he'd made up his mind. So they tried to pick their fights and keep personal relationships in as good a shape as possible. A lot of active diplomacy took place around and under Trump.[159]

The Australian achievement in managing Trump was conspicuous. The credit goes to Morrison and Turnbull, followed by Joe Hockey as Australia's ambassador to the United States.

Biden's elevation to the presidency in January 2021 changed the equation, with the new leader embracing support for US allies, the Indo-Pacific concept, a firm stance on China, climate change action and multilateralism. This agenda created opportunities and risks for Morrison. Biden, unlike Trump, would run a functioning administration. While Biden would say the right things to allies, the evidence pointed to a foreign policy geared to domestic calculations.

The August 2021 withdrawal from Afghanistan, when Biden said the era of 'forever' wars was over and implemented Trump's agreement with the Taliban, highlighted the shifting US strategic outlook. While his argument to quit an unpopular 20-year war had its justification, Biden was explicit in rejecting major overseas troop deployments and embracing a narrower focus on core US national security interests. Biden signalled a shift in priorities to the Indo-Pacific, a signal welcomed by Morrison. The bigger question, however, was whether the United States was retreating from foreign commitments so that it could repair its internal fractures.

It is easy to forget the risk Trump posed to the Australia–US partnership. As an outsider who repudiated the model of US global leadership since the Second World War – arguing the cost-benefit equation no longer worked in America's favour – Trump would have been a danger if he had taken a set against Australia. He had questioned the value of the North Atlantic Treaty Organization (NATO), cast doubt on the US–Japan security partnership, engaged in a trade war with China and criticised allied European leaders. Trump–Turnbull relations had hovered in a fog of uncertainty after an initial acrimonious phone call over an agreement for the United States to resettle refugees held on Nauru and Manus Island in Papua New Guinea in exchange for Australia agreeing to take Central American refugees.

After their meeting in New York, Turnbull concluded that Trump's foreign policy perspective was 'isolationist' and 'dystopian' – 'everyone hated each other [and] had done for centuries'.[160] Equally dangerous for Australia was Trump's trade policy ignorance – his view that if America had a bilateral trade deficit with another country then the United States was the trade loser. Trump loathed the liberal global trading system that Australia relied upon and backed so firmly, his protectionism being a 40-year-old prejudice impervious to argument.

Morrison inherited an impressive record from Turnbull. On the two bilateral tests that counted – the refugee agreement and Australian exemptions on the tariffs to protect his steel and aluminium industries – Trump delivered. Turnbull also inherited in Hockey an ambassador who understood Trump. Hockey's folksy creativity was a success exemplified in his '100 years of mateship' theme, a sentimental pitch to the Australian–American bond forged in fighting together in every major conflict since the First World War.

Morrison's first rule in dealing with Trump was caution. He never made the mistake other leaders did of indulging in public criticisms of the president. 'It was not my job to join in any international commentary on the guy,' Morrison said.[161] The pressure to criticise was enormous, reaching its zenith when Trump gave legitimacy to the invasion of the Capitol in January 2021, with the Labor Party and commentators calling on Morrison to condemn Trump. Morrison never wavered from his principle.

The initial Trump–Morrison meeting was a 20-minute catch-up on the sidelines of the G20 leaders' meeting in Argentina in December 2018. It was a difficult summit for Morrison – he had to explain to Trump what had happened to Turnbull, and he was a stranger among mainly established leaders. 'We've just gotten to know each other and so far, so good,' Trump told the media.

Their next encounters sealed a personal affinity. The pivotal event was Morrison's re-election in May 2019 as a conservative leader defying progressive opponents. Trump saw Morrison as a fellow traveller, and he loved political winners.

'Donald always knew one thing about you,' Morrison said.

> And that's what defined your relationship with him. If he talked about Mike Pompeo, it was first in his class at West Point. And [Treasury Secretary] Steve Mnuchin – the only guy to make money in Hollywood. He would fixate on one thing about you, positive or negative . . . after I won the election, he couldn't leave it. He was one of the first to ring me and he was just over the moon.[162]

In June, the month after the election, Morrison visited the United Kingdom to attend the seventy-fifth anniversary celebrations commemorating the D-Day landing at Normandy. He described Trump's behaviour during a lunch at Portsmouth: 'We're sitting around this table and Donald stops and says "this guy, this guy, he's the biggest winner at this table, he's a bigger winner than all of us." And I'm sitting there trying to be respectful to the room and Donald's going off like this.' Trump had his defining idea about Morrison – 'he's [Morrison] gone and won an election against the odds, just like I did'.[163]

The affinity was on display again in late June 2019 when, on the eve of the G20 meeting in Osaka, Trump and Morrison dined together. Sitting opposite each other at the 75-minute dinner with their respective teams of officials, Trump and Morrison canvassed Australian domestic politics, the role of the 'quiet Australians', global trade and the US–China trade battle. The US side included Pompeo, Mnuchin and National Security Adviser John Bolton.[164]

'He [Trump] asked for the dinner in Osaka,' Morrison said. Morrison believed Trump must have been briefed on Australia's policy of turning back asylum seeker vessels at sea, which Morrison had overseen as Immigration Minister. 'He was fascinated by it . . . and I said "that's right" and I explained it all to him . . . he went, "This guy knows how to solve some really weird problems, I'm trying to build a wall, and how did you do this?"'[165]

But Morrison knew nothing could be assumed with Trump. It was important that Morrison had met Vice President Pence before meeting the president, having held talks with Pence in Port Moresby in mid-November 2018 during the Asia-Pacific Economic Cooperation (APEC) summit.

Morrison's view of the alliance is conventional, pragmatic and centred on national interests. But while Morrison's approach to the United States is likened to that of John Howard's, the generational and historical differences are significant. Howard belonged to a different age. His historical memory was the Second World War and his lived experience was the Cold War. Howard entered the parliament in 1974 and Morrison in 2007, a full 33 years later.

Howard carried the emotional and strategic faiths of the pro-US 'greatest generation' ingrained as a way of life, while Morrison's experience is different – he lacks the emotional bond with the United States typified by figures such as Howard and Kim Beazley. Morrison would never say it, but he sees Australia as a superior, more cohesive society than America. Morrison came to the prime ministership not to reshape the US alliance, but to find how best it could be used. He saw the alliance as a cost-benefit gain for

Australia in security terms and that his task was to secure the best possible relationship with Trump and Biden.

Managing Trump was tricky precisely because Trump identified Morrison as a fellow traveller – but this was not the case. Morrison, unlike Trump, was a political insider, a conventional party leader, a centrist and a pragmatist. Moreover, the Trump– Morrison period saw policy differences between America and Australia that were some of the most significant in the past several decades: disagreement over the liberal trade system and the WTO, Trump's protectionism, his globally disruptive trade war with China, the Trans-Pacific Partnership trade deal, the Paris Agreement on climate, the Iran nuclear deal, the Human Rights Council, the WHO and the ideological framing of the contest with China.

The key was the absence of a core security dispute. Yet the differences highlighted how much the United States was drifting away from responsible global leadership towards 'America First' positions that undermined the rules-based order.

Morrison's ability to manage Trump was materially assisted by the Australian media. Its obsession with depicting Morrison as pandering to Trump meant it rarely emphasised such differences and helped to keep them below the radar. But Morrison's unwise decision to appear with Trump at what became a political rally in Ohio in September 2019 only invited suggestions that they were fellow travellers.

Meanwhile, Morrison inherited a government system that was alert to the shift in the global power balance, but still confident about the United States. The 2017 Foreign Policy White Paper said:

> In the United States, there is greater debate about the costs of sustaining its global leadership ... Since 1950, the United States' share of the global economy has nearly halved from 27 per cent to 15 per cent today (in purchasing power parity terms). This contrasts with China's rapid increase, growing from 2 per cent in 1980 to nearly 18 per cent today ... China's power and influence are growing to match, and in some cases exceed, that of the United States ... Even as China's power grows and it competes more directly with the United States regionally and globally, the United States will, for the foreseeable future, retain its significant global lead in military and soft power ... The Australian government judges that the United States' long-term interests will anchor its economic and security engagement in the Indo-Pacific.[166]

In the four years since 2017, doubts surrounding the US capacity to shape the region and balance

China have only grown. This is seeded in Australia's bureaucratic system – a change from the Howard–Bush era where mutual confidence ran high.

Asked if he shared the diagnosis about US decline, Morrison says:

I don't share it. It's an obvious fact that America's relative economic power has changed; that's just a fact because of the development of the global economy. And its military relative authority has changed because of growth in other parts of the world. [But] if you look at America's history, honestly, they tear themselves apart on a regular basis and then they always get stronger.[167]

This reflects a visceral faith in the United States and the sheer depth of Australia's ties to the alliance. Peter Varghese says:

America is changing, that's obvious. There are more doubts about American reliability. Trump showed the US could move in unpredictable ways. Biden's election does not erase these doubts. But the relevance of the US alliance will remain. The benefits in the alliance flow to Australia from the deterrent effect on potential enemies, access to defence equipment and intelligence and shared values. Those benefits are going to keep flowing. No Australian government will want to lose them.[168]

In his approach to the alliance, Morrison has two personas: he invariably invokes sentimentality, but he typically brings pragmatic commitment to the task. At the seventieth anniversary of the ANZUS alliance, Morrison said he regarded the treaty as the 'greatest achievement' of the Menzies government. He described it as 'mates helping mates' based on free economies and free peoples who 'see the world through the same lens'.[169]

After 70 years, the alliance has become a political and bureaucratic institution in its own right. It exists at the level of bipartisan political commitment, military and intelligence links, joint facilities, defence industry integration, high-tech cooperation underpinned by a sprawling investment foundation and networks of people.

The vision Morrison brings to the alliance involves more depth and greater width. He envisages the alliance deepening into cooperation over defence technology, space, cyber, supply chains, vaccine cooperation, missile defence and precision weapons. 'We're going deeper,' he says of the partnership.[170] But Morrison also has an expansive view of the alliance in the region – he sees Australia and

America working within the Quad, and alongside Pacific and Southeast Asian nations to help secure a balance of power that favours freedom.

Morrison's ambition to 'renew and modernise' ANZUS went to new heights in 2021[171] with the AUKUS nuclear-powered submarine initiative between Australia, the United Kingdom and United States. This testified to Morrison's faith in America and a deepening of the strategic intimacy that defied sceptics who argued that American domestic political fractures made it a dangerously less reliable senior partner.

The powerful presence of the alliance, its cost-benefit dividends, its huge infrastructure and the abiding sense of confidence it generated in America meant Morrison, like all his predecessors, had no interest in running a 'distancing' strategy as insurance against a US reliability retreat. Previous prime ministers have all looked to renew and re-invent the alliance, rather than distance Australia from it.

However, a deepening theme in public commentary is that Australia is blind to decisive changes in America's outlook. Hugh White has warned for a decade that Australia's security assumptions are dissolving in American uncertainty:

The reasons go deeper than the failure of the Trump administration. They go to the fundamental question of whether America needs to preserve its leadership role in Asia enough to justify the costs and risks of containing a rival as powerful as China in China's own backyard. American voters may be even less keen. So, even after the pandemic, and even after a more effective president than Trump, America's ability to contain China's ambitions in Asia and ensure Australia's security over the decades to come can no longer be taken for granted.[172]

White also says:

US forces remain more powerful overall, but China has many advantages in the Western Pacific – fighting a defensive campaign close to home bases ... The US can no longer expect a swift, cheap victory in a war with China ... it must expect a long and very costly war – bigger than anything since Vietnam and probably bigger than any war since 1945 with no clear prospect of ultimate victory.[173]

Historian and student of the alliance James Curran says:

Both major parties appear incapable of meeting the reality of a less committed United States. Australian political elites have spent the best part of a decade in denial about persistent racial, cultural and socio-economic currents in American politics which – short of war – will dominate any White House.

Curran says Australia's attitude towards the US alliance is anchored in images of the Second World War and the Cold War – times that have passed. It is failing to adjust to a different America.[174]

Geoff Raby warns that Australia is now 'joined to the US hip in a way that hasn't happened since the Cold War' and it must now assess 'how far down the path of competition with China it is prepared to go'.[175] Allan Gyngell says, 'The problem we face with the United States at the moment is that so much of the challenge in America is an internal challenge and so much of the focus of the administration is domestic. We have a deep relationship with the US . . . but I don't think it's the same as it's been in the past.'[176]

These are powerful critiques. But they neither sketch out a viable alternative policy nor confront the real choices an Australian prime minister such as Morrison faces in office. No prime minister would lightly downgrade or hedge on the US alliance at the precise time China is flexing its muscles. The idea that China would offer Australia anything for distancing itself from the United States is fanciful. What is Australia supposed to get in return?

This is never adequately explained. No prime minister, moreover, would base policy on the likelihood of Beijing establishing primacy in the region, since that is a contestable outcome and contrary to Australia's interest. The judgment that successive prime ministers have made is that the lesser gamble lies in staying close with America. Even given future uncertainty over whether the United States might remain a robust force or might be limited by internal traumas, the country will remain the leading military power for some years yet.

Former ambassador to the United States and former DFAT chief Dennis Richardson says:

> I don't think the alliance is really dependent on personalities. Personalities can impact on the day-to-day and the atmospherics. But the alliance has never been held hostage to one personality and that was the case during the Trump presidency and would be the case in the future.[177]

After his 2019 re-election, Morrison said the US alliance had 'never been stronger' and provided Australia with 'irreplaceable hard power capabilities and intelligence'. But Morrison's conception of the alliance fused with his notion of Australian sovereignty. Post-election, his message to the Trump administration was: 'Australia will continue to pull its weight.'[178]

Morrison was alert to Trump's demand that allies do more. Trump's message was that America would no longer pay the price of global leadership, yet he insisted its pre-eminence would remain. Morrison's response was to offer more self-reliance within the US partnership. As is his habit, Morrison coined a slogan for his stance: 'We look to the US, but we don't leave it to the US.'[179]

Self-reliance is an old idea, periodically recycled. It had a profound impact on Australia's thinking from 1969 onwards when President Richard Nixon spoke at Guam, warning that other nations must assume prime responsibility for their defence. The Nixon Doctrine was the spur to Australia moving from a strategy of 'forward defence' to self-reliance and the defence of Australia in the 1987 Defence White Paper.[180]

Greater self-reliance made sense with Trump and beyond Trump. It is obvious given the two trends: an assertive China, and a less predictable America. 'Every argument points to the need for more Australian self-reliance,' says Peter Varghese. 'The US will be expecting more from Australia as an alliance partner and the demands from a dynamic region give self-reliance an even greater salience.'[181]

Morrison put his pitch to Trump on the South Lawn of the White House during his state visit in September 2019, a symbolic occasion involving a state dinner, the first for an Australian prime minister since John Howard in 2006 and only the second of the Trump administration. After affirming the shared values of the two nations, Morrison said, 'Mr President, Australia may often look to the United States, but we have never been a country that has been prepared to leave it to the United States. We don't, that's not our way. We pull our weight . . . you won't find a more sure and steadfast friend, a better mate, than Australia.'[182]

Morrison told the author: 'I was trying to find a way to really encapsulate the nature of our relationship – it wasn't specific to Trump and could have been any president . . . I was trying to get at: why is Australia's relationship with the United States different to everyone else's?'

The question implies that Australia has a deeper relationship with the United States than other allies, a view many would contest. Nevertheless, it is the assumption that led him to launch the AUKUS initiative. Morrison's argument, that Australia is prepared to 'do a lot of the heavy lifting', is rhetorically convenient, only partly true and invites the United States to lodge higher demands on Australia.[183]

Upon his return from America, Morrison said the alliance was 'our past, our present and our future'.[184]

In his 2020 Defence Update, Morrison announced a defence budget trajectory beyond two per cent of GDP, combined with a strategic revamp based on force projection; that is, the ability to meet adversaries at distance from Australia. Australia would make a greater effort to ensure its own security within the more tightly defined priority area of the Indo-Pacific. While arguing that the Update would advance Australian sovereignty, Morrison also said that 'it will make us a better and more efficient ally'. Morrison envisaged an 'ever closer alliance' operating in conjunction with regional neighbours.[185]

But Mike Pompeo was keeping Australia under pressure. At the 2019 Australia–United States Ministerial Consultations (AUSMIN) meeting in Sydney, Pompeo pushed for Australia's support against China on the trade and security fronts. Declaring the alliance 'unbreakable', Pompeo escalated US demands. In a famous statement about Australia's trade with China, he said, 'Look, you can sell your soul for a pile of soy beans or you can protect your people.' Pompeo said the capacity of the People's Liberation Army 'to do exactly what they are doing' was the direct result of Beijing's unfair trade activity. In short, the trade conflict and the security conflict were inseparable.[186]

This was not Australia's position. Australia's national interest was to uphold its trade relationship with China, not sign on to Trump's bilateral trade retaliation. Here was Morrison's dilemma: deepening ties with a Trump administration meant repudiating past US leadership norms that had served Australia well.

In his lavish 2019 White House welcome, Morrison was successful in juggling these competing interests. The test came during the prolonged Trump–Morrison media conference, one of the most difficult any prime minister has faced with a US president in years. Sitting next to Trump, Morrison said, 'We have a comprehensive strategic partnership with China. We work well with China . . . [its] growth has been great for Australia. But we need to make sure that we all compete on the same playing field.'[187]

The position Morrison took was that Trump's complaints about China's unfair trade and technological practices were 'legitimate'. Indeed, Morrison told his ministers that Trump had done the world a favour by calling out China's tactics. But in Washington and Chicago, Morrison separated himself from the United States by saying Australia had 'always welcomed' China's economic growth.[188] 'Australia and the US come at this from a different perspective,' Morrison said. 'We have a trade surplus with China. You [America] have a trade deficit . . . that is, I think, going to affect the lens through which you see China and its economic success.' He had been 'supportive' of Trump's effort to strike a new deal with China.[189]

Morrison wanted an end to the US–China trade war. But he broke from Trump on the solution, saying it was 'important' that US–China trade disputes were resolved 'in a way that is WTO consistent and does not undermine the interests of other parties, including Australia'.[190]

The government's willingness to draw the line publicly against the United States was apparent at the 2020 AUSMIN meeting in Washington, DC, which Foreign Minister Payne had called the 'most significant' in her time. The meeting had been preceded by Pompeo's speech at the Richard Nixon Presidential Library injecting ideological warfare into the US–China disputes. Pompeo quoted Nixon, saying that 'the world cannot be safe until China changes'. He asserted that 'blind engagement' with China had failed, the upshot being that Beijing had sent its 'propagandists into our press conferences, our research centres, our high schools, our colleges, and even into our PTA meetings'. Pompeo said the 'biggest lie' was that the Communist Party spoke for 1.4 billion Chinese who are 'surveilled, oppressed and scared'. China could no longer be treated as a normal law-abiding country and free nations 'must induce China to change'. Washington's intent was 'to engage and to empower the Chinese people, a dynamic, freedom-loving people', to reject the Communist Party, and he called upon free nations 'to act'.[191]

Great powers like the United States can take such a position, but not Australia. Payne came under intense pressure from the Americans at this meeting but repudiated their efforts at tougher language on China.

Asked about Pompeo's speech at the AUSMIN press conference, Payne said:

We make our own decisions, our own judgments in the Australian national interest ... so we deal with China in the same way, we have a strong economic engagement, other engagement, and it works in the interests of both countries. That said, of course, we don't agree on everything. We are very different countries, we are very different systems ... As my Prime Minister put it recently, the relationship that we have with China is important, and we have no intention of injuring it, but nor do we intend to do things that are contrary to our interests.

Payne said Australia and America did not 'agree on everything', and that was part of a 'respectful relationship'.[192]

Pompeo's speech highlighted the potential for Australia–US differences over China. Launching a frontal assault on the Chinese Communist Party had no place in any rational Australian policy, but it revealed how Australia needed to be quarantined from conservative American ideology.

Morrison's private assessment is that he influenced the Trump administration more than it influenced him. Certainly his management of Trump – a task that could have backfired – was a success. Varghese says Morrison was 'effective', aware that his job was to uphold the alliance without succumbing to 'Trump derangement syndrome'.[193]

The alacrity with which Morrison moved to establish personal links with President Biden was almost impolite. As usual, Morrison was optimistic, searching for common bonds and playing down differences. He told the author he felt a 'strong alignment' with Biden in the president's support for liberal democracy and his commitment to the Indo-Pacific.[194]

Morrison took heart from their first post-election phone call on 12 November 2020. He took more heart when new Secretary of State Antony Blinken said America's relationship with China would be 'competitive when it should be, collaborative when it can be and adversarial when it must be'. This seemed to be a grown-up government.

The big step was Biden's March 2021 convening of the first meeting of the Quad at head-of-government level with the leaders of the United States, Australia, Japan and India coming together by video link. Morrison saw it as a vindication of Australia's diplomacy and tangible evidence that Biden understood the need for the United States to play a robust and balancing regional role against China. For Morrison, there could not have been a better start to the Biden administration. He told the author he was 'thrilled' by Biden's moves.[195]

The government was further delighted when the President's Indo-Pacific coordinator Kurt Campbell said the United States had told China it was not prepared to improve relations while 'a close and dear ally is being subjected to a form of economic coercion', a reference to the tariffs and other trade measures China had imposed on Australia since May 2020. Campbell said the United States would not take 'substantial steps' to improve relations with Beijing while Australia was the subject of punitive action. He said Biden had told Morrison during the Quad meeting that 'we stood together on this'.[196]

The Morrison government appreciated the reassurance. Yet it may have been more cosmetic than real. How tenable was this linkage? How viable was it to think the United States would not improve China ties until Beijing had resolved the Australia trade issue? The government's initial reaction seemed to reflect a naïve acceptance of Campbell's assurances.

A few months later, Campbell said China was displaying a 'harshness' that seemed 'unyielding' in its dealings with Australia, suggesting he did not think any concessions were likely soon. Campbell, who knows Australia well, said relations between Washington and Canberra were 'deepening', while noting that 'these are not completely like-minded governments'. It was a timely caution.[197]

Unlike Morrison, Biden is communicating with China. Linda Jakobson says:

Great powers like the United States can get away with changing their policy towards China, but Australia won't be accorded that luxury. The situation now is that Australia has no political dialogue with

China while the US and China continue to have the highest dialogue.[198]

This is a dangerous situation for Australia. Does it depend upon the United States for information about China? The risk is that Australia will be disadvantaged by deals the United States and China will strike and by the trade-offs they negotiate. Any long-run perpetuation of this situation is unacceptable for Australia.

After Trump, Biden's language seemed reassuring: 'America is back. Diplomacy is back at the centre of our foreign policy.'[199] But Biden's foreign policy outlook was steeped in Democratic Party orthodoxy, reinforced by a supreme pledge to renew the American heartland. The mission of the Biden presidency was enshrined in his inaugural address – it was to repair, restore and heal. This suggested the healing process at home might have priority over foreign commitments, apart from core threats to US security. Biden's domestic agenda was daunting: fighting a 'once-in-a-century' virus, rebuilding the American middle class, confronting climate change and defeating racism and extremism.[200]

This was not necessarily a comfortable fit with Morrison's Australia. On climate change, the international campaign Biden would run through his envoy, John Kerry, helped to convince Morrison he must shift Australia towards net zero emissions by 2050. For Biden, climate change action was a faith. The president would assess leaders by their willingness to address what he branded an 'existential' challenge. While Morrison in October 2021 won a decisive change in the Coalition's position to accept net zero emissions by 2050, this would not satisfy the United States. Its main goal was to persuade nations to adopt more ambitious targets for 2030. The upshot is that Morrison faces permanent tension with the Biden administration over climate change. His best hope is to limit the criticism. The bigger issue is the extent to which Biden allows dissatisfaction on climate change to affect wider relations.

There are other differences. Biden has given every sign of sticking by most of Trump's trade protection agenda. And Morrison rejected much of the Northern Hemisphere orthodoxy about a bigger role for government in economic recovery, declaring the need for 'a business-led recovery, not a government-centred' recovery.[201]

Biden's withdrawal from Afghanistan on 30 August 2021 revealed his determination to shift the contours of US strategic policy. His acceptance of the Taliban victory reflected two convictions: that the war in Afghanistan should have been abandoned many years earlier, and that American reliance on military intervention to remake nations must be rejected as a mission.

'After 20 years of war in Afghanistan, I refused to send another generation of America's sons and daughters to fight a war that should have ended long ago,' Biden said. 'The decision about Afghanistan is not just about Afghanistan. It's about ending an era of major military operations to remake other countries.' Seeking to move beyond the 20-year saga of Iraq and Afghanistan, Biden said that 'we've been a nation at war too long'.[202] The withdrawal was a Trump–Biden project – proof of the extent to which these political rivals were driven by the same domestic conclusions.

Biden said quitting Afghanistan meant a reprioritising to meet the China challenge. At face value, this was good news for Australia. Morrison felt the Afghanistan withdrawal, despite the final chaos and the consequences of a Taliban victory, constituted a necessary rebalancing for the United States. 'At some point, the United States had to say: "How long do we remain there and for what ends?"' Morrison was confident the upshot meant 'increasing the US focus on the Indo-Pacific'.[203] This was Biden's message. 'We're engaged in a serious competition with China,' he said.

The deeper question revolves around Biden's character. The debacle of the Afghanistan withdrawal inevitably raises doubts about US resolve, prompting allies to worry yet again and inviting questions about Biden's strength. It poses questions about whether this is a president tough enough to lead America in its deepening strategic competition with China.

The historical message from the alliance is its adaptability during periods of strategic upheaval. There are mixed omens about Morrison–Biden ties and the extent of their personal rapport, but Morrison is an optimist about US relations under Biden. He sees the alliance and its infrastructure as reflecting not just shared national security interests but an instinctual link, almost a moral bond, between the two nations. In Morrison's view, the US alliance is a fusion between national interest pragmatism and shared moral values.

CHAPTER SEVEN

Navigating the Indo-Pacific

At 8.32 am Washington time on 12 March 2021, US President Joe Biden convened the first virtual summit of four leaders from Indo-Pacific democracies, aspiring to recast the terms of strategic competition with China. Scott Morrison told the Quad summit that this was 'a partnership of strategic trust, of common hope and shared values'.[204] Biden's initiative reflected a long-emerging but suddenly erupting common purpose among different nations driven by China's behaviour. It was an opportunity for Morrison to realise his deepest foreign policy aspirations.

This was the first multilateral summit hosted by Biden as president. He articulated its goal in the well-known phrase, 'a free and open Indo-Pacific', which he said was 'essential' to 'each of our futures'. The resulting statement from the four leaders – Biden,

Morrison, Japan's Prime Minister Yoshihide Suga and India's Prime Minister Narendra Modi – pledged to an Indo-Pacific governed by international law, principles of freedom and peaceful resolution of disputes. The leaders wanted political choices 'free from coercion' and said 'in recent years that vision has increasingly been tested' – a reference to China.

Biden's convening of the Quad at leaders' level represented the culmination of strategic decisions in each of the four nations. But the American authorisation was decisive. It followed a long campaign by Japan's previous prime minister Shinzo Abe and was the goal Morrison had sought in his personal diplomacy during 2020.

For Morrison, the Quad assumed a status greater than its reality at the time. His focus was on its potential. The Quad was emblematic of the central themes he was pursuing: a deeper US institutional tie to the Indo-Pacific, closer strategic coordination with Japan and India, a framework to balance and contest China's behaviour, and a belief that Indo-Pacific nations working together were not just pawns in the US–China power competition but could influence their own future.

In an interview, Morrison said, 'Why is the Quad important? It enables us to build sovereign capability. It enhances our agency significantly within the region. And it reinforces the principles of the liberal world order. It ticks every single one of these boxes.'[205]

To Morrison's mind, the Quad is an instrument to help resolve the historical Australian dilemma of having interests unable to be realised by its capacities. The Quad is the latest event in the perpetual Australian diplomacy of joining coalitions of interest – witness the APEC leaders' meeting, the East Asia Summit and the Trans-Pacific Partnership, among others. Morrison sees the Quad as a force multiplier. It will help Australia achieve what it cannot achieve alone. Its long-run strategic significance is to act as a check on China.

In August 2021, former prime minister Kevin Rudd said Beijing had now 'concluded that the Quad represents one of the most consequential challenges to Chinese ambition in the years ahead'. Rudd highlighted the Quad's role in undermining President Xi Jinping's strategy by 'unifying a multilateral coalition of resistance' against his aspiration 'to make China the world's top economic, technological and potentially even military power'.[206] The lingering question is how China will seek to undermine the Quad.

While Japan rightly felt a sense of authorship of the Quad, efforts were quickly underway in 2021 to install the idea in the pantheon of Australian diplomatic feats. 'This is a project that our government has championed,' Morrison said.[207] His sense of ownership was palpable, but exaggerated. In his opening statement to the summit, he called it 'a new dawn in the Indo-Pacific'. He later called the meeting 'a whole new level of cooperation'. Days later, Morrison told government MPs there were 'things that happen in the life of a government that transcend the generations . . . This is, I would argue, the most significant thing to have occurred to protect Australia's security and sovereignty since ANZUS.' For most analysts, this was conspicuous hyperbole.

Beyond the hyperbole, the Quad offered some of the best insights into Morrison's thinking. He wanted more collaboration from major regional nations – Japan and India – and tighter links between the region and the United States. Morrison had lobbied Mike Pompeo on the Quad and felt it would have come to fruition under Trump had he been re-elected. Upon Biden's victory, Morrison moved quickly to coordinate joint Australia–Japan messages to the new White House. Views in Australia about the Quad invariably mirrored views about China: the more pessimistic about China, the more optimistic about the Quad.

Former Australian ambassador to Japan Bruce Miller says:

The Quad leaders' meeting has come into being after a lengthy and difficult gestation, precisely because of China's actions and its alienating diplomacy. Without that, we would have seen the same half-hearted commitments to the Quad, or lack of focus that has marked its journey over the last 15 years. If China persists with its current stance, then the Quad will drive ever closer security cooperation between the four. If China moderates its behaviour and its rhetoric, unlikely though that may appear for now, then the Quad will matter less.[208]

Endorsing the initiative, Peter Varghese says:

Our strategy with China should be to 'engage and constrain'. Australia has no option in a strategic sense but to work with our partners – the US, Japan, India and others – to push back when China behaves in unacceptable ways. We have to make leverage a two-way street. Morrison's diplomacy on the Quad has been well judged, but we need to appreciate the Quad has its limits.[209]

There had been a long Australian pathway to the Quad. Alexander Downer as foreign minister had pushed for a trilateral dialogue involving the United States, Japan and Australia. It had its first leaders' meeting in Sydney in 2007 with President George W. Bush, Shinzo Abe and John Howard. An adviser said, 'The main subject discussed was how to bring India into play.' Downer called the 2021 Quad leaders' summit 'a major moment in Australian foreign policy'.[210]

Integral to the process has been Australia's embrace of the Indo-Pacific concept, an evolution from 'Asia-Pacific'. Former foreign minister Julie Bishop told the author she regarded her distinctive achievement as minister to be her championing of the concept 'of the Indo-Pacific as Australia's sphere of influence' and the promotion of it 'not just as a geographical term, but as a geostrategic/geopolitical term'.[211] The embrace of the concept by the United States and much of the region reflected deep forces at work.

Australian advocate Rory Medcalf says:

> The term recognises that both economic ties and strategic competition now encompass an expansive two ocean region due in large part to China's ascent and that other countries must protect their interests through new partnerships across the blurring of old geographical boundaries.

Medcalf says the concept has many identities – it is characterised as America's bid to thwart China,

India's play for greatness, Japan's plan to regain influence, and Australia's focus on alliance building. Yet, he says, it is more driven by China's expanding economic, political and military presence across two oceans.[212]

In Morrison's view, the Quad unites democracies (including two US alliance partners), deepens Australia's links with two regional economic giants and widens the arc of our interests from the Indian to Pacific oceans. Uppermost in his mind is checking China's capacity for economic and strategic coercion. Morrison says the Quad further ensures that 'Australia is not acting in isolation and that Australia cannot be isolated.' The Quad strengthens what he calls a 'web of influence . . . It helps us shape the region in a way that protects, defends and nurtures Australia's interests.' It promotes 'a rules-based order in the Indo-Pacific'.[213]

Morrison sees the Quad as demonstrating that regional nations can exert collective influence in their own right. He says Australia does not want its future determined by 'stark choices' in a US–China contest or to have its sovereignty undermined in US–China rivalry. He says Australia has its 'own views as an independent sovereign state' and its preference is to avoid being 'forced into binary choices'. Morrison says 'greater latitude will be required from the world's largest powers to accommodate the individual interests of their partners and allies'.[214]

In his 2020 book on the Indo-Pacific concept, Medcalf pursues this theme. The future of Asia, he argues, is not just about China. His subtitle is: 'Why China won't map the future'. Medcalf says that by 2050, four Asian nations – India, Japan, Australia and Indonesia – will eclipse China in combined population and GDP. 'The picture of middle players as potent balancers becomes starker still,' Medcalf says. As more nations become its champions, the Indo-Pacific concept could gain greater purpose, though Medcalf concedes that this depends on leadership, diplomacy and collective action.[215]

In his 2020 and 2021 remarks, Morrison heads in this direction. He talks of the need for Indo-Pacific nations to work in concert and 'create deeper habits of cooperation' on economic and security issues. Two themes occur repeatedly in Morrison's speeches on the subject: the need for a 'strategic balance' in the Indo-Pacific, and the need for 'agreed rules and norms'. He says the Quad constitutes a 'positive message' for the region and for ASEAN.

How might the Quad evolve? Whether it can deliver on such optimism remains unknown. There are many sceptics. The four nations involved have different histories, cultures, outlooks and geographies. How far they can work together remains to be tested. It is extremely unlikely that the Quad will become a military alliance. It is not going to become an Asian NATO. Morrison is not thinking like that. Yet senior security advisers in his government want the Quad to aggregate power and, in the words of one influential figure, 'become a quasi-alliance without security guarantees'.

The Quad's arrival at leaders' level should mean an effort to impose costs on China for bad behaviour. But Hugh White issues a warning: 'China won't be constrained by diplomacy alone.' He argues that China's rise is tied to military power. Regional nations want to avoid Chinese hegemony, but they are unlikely to risk the dangers of a military alliance against China.[216]

It is early days. Signs are that the Quad's foundations are firm in the United States, where there is bipartisan support. It is part of Biden's 'tough on China' outlook. Its future will depend heavily on India, because India is not a security partner of the United States. The working rule on which Morrison operates is to 'only progress the Quad at the pace of the slowest member'.[217] One test of the Quad's success is whether it might attract not just regional supporters, but new members.

In practical terms, the Quad leaders' summit focused on the pandemic. Heads of government agreed to assist production and distribution of one billion vaccine doses in the Indo-Pacific, establish a Quad Vaccine Experts Group and prioritise health outcomes. Australia's contribution to this effort was $100 million. Leaders identified climate change, new technologies, cyber challenges and deeper cooperation with Southeast Asian nations as priorities. The intention is to show the Quad's capacity to produce public goods as an alternative to China.

Morrison's aspirations for the Quad fused with his drive for enhanced bilateral ties with Japan and India. With Japanese Prime Minister Abe, Morrison inherited a relationship of trust established by Tony Abbott and Malcolm Turnbull. Morrison was the beneficiary of Abe's vision – Abe saw that China's emergence would drive Japan and Australia closer together. Abe was a valuable asset for Liberal prime ministers seeking deeper bilateral security ties, given his effort to move Japan beyond its post-war constitution, which limited its military capacity to self-defence.

Three months after becoming Prime Minister, Morrison met Abe in Darwin for the first time. It was an emotional occasion – the first visit by a Japanese Prime Minister to the city since Japan's bombing of Darwin during the Second World War. The leaders laid wreaths at the war memorial. Abe said the nations had achieved reconciliation and had become 'special strategic partners'. Morrison believed the leaders had established a personal connection.[218] They agreed to press ahead to conclude a Reciprocal Access Agreement (RAA).

This became the focus of Morrison's diplomacy with Japan. He was following a strong Liberal tradition, most recently embodied by Abbott who, identifying Abe as a fellow conservative, had sought a closer security relationship between the two nations. While Abbott's central initiative to acquire Japanese submarines failed, the two nations agreed to consider the RAA following a proposal put forward by Foreign Minister Bishop in 2014.

Morrison and Abe met in June 2019 when Morrison visited Japan for the G20 summit, and the two leaders held a virtual meeting in July 2020 that canvassed the pandemic, the Indo-Pacific, support for the Quad and the strategic partnership. Abe's surprise resignation in August 2020 and the elevation of his ally and former cabinet secretary Yoshihide Suga as Prime Minister gave Morrison an even greater sense of urgency. He proceeded with a long-planned visit to Japan despite the quarantine restrictions he would face on return. This was the first overseas visit Morrison made during the pandemic, and he became the first foreign leader to meet Suga on home soil.

Morrison told officials that the RAA must be ready for authorisation and that it would frame the visit. His aim was to ensure Australia and Japan sent the same messages about the Quad to Biden as incoming president. In Tokyo, Suga announced the RAA deal and Morrison called it 'a landmark defence treaty', another exaggeration. The RAA makes it easier for Australia's military to deploy to Japan, particularly for emergency assistance, and facilitates bilateral military movements. Its practical value is streamlining military cooperation and its symbolic value is signalling Australia–Japan alignment in the context of China. It is Japan's first agreement covering foreign forces on its territory since its earlier agreement with the United States. But it is no treaty alliance with security guarantees. Still, Morrison branded the RAA a 'pivotal moment in the history of Japan–Australia ties'.

Bonding with Japan, the world's third largest economy and the main infrastructure provider to the region, strengthens Australia's options. The joint statement from the leaders was conspicuous for expressing 'serious concerns' about the situation in the South China Sea, ongoing militarisation, and 'coercive or unilateral' efforts to change the status quo, reflecting a shared critique of Beijing.[219] Morrison said establishing a personal relationship with Suga was one reason 'why it was so important to come', noting it was 'no small thing' for a prime minister to visit in the middle of a pandemic. Obviously, Morrison was disappointed at Suga's resignation in 2021 due to domestic political pressures.

As for enhanced ties with India, Morrison had several meetings with Prime Minister Narendra Modi at summits during 2018 and 2019. He was scheduled to make a major visit to India in 2020 but that was postponed due to the pandemic. They held a virtual summit that June with relations upgraded to a comprehensive strategic partnership and a far more tangible agenda of collaborative ventures. In 2020, India invited Australia to participate in the annual Malabar naval exercises, a further sign of rapport. This coincided with deepening Indian perceptions that China was a hostile power, a bonus for Australia, though it would be folly to ever think India could rival or balance China in its own right. Morrison and Modi had further talks in 2021, and in April Morrison spoke by video at the annual Raisina Dialogue, his theme being the common values and shared strategic interests of Australia and India in a region consumed by competition.[220]

The Quad has irritated Beijing, but whether it changes China's behaviour remains an open question. The pivotal issue is whether the rest of the region sees the Quad as useful and positive. The four Quad members are such different nations that doubts about the group will not easily dissipate. Morrison has raised expectations about the Quad's ability to deliver tangible benefits to the region. It will need to show those credentials as a prelude to its bigger job of restraining Chinese power.

CHAPTER EIGHT

Morrison and AUKUS

On the morning of Thursday 16 September 2021 (AEST), Scott Morrison appeared in a virtual event with Boris Johnson and Joe Biden to announce an elevated trilateral security partnership. Essentially an enhanced defence technology agreement, its first initiative was an in-principle decision to deliver a nuclear-powered submarine fleet for Australia. Called AUKUS, the agreement was a path-breaking step for each nation, with regional and global significance.

The agreement was the culmination of Morrison's national security and foreign policy strategy as Prime Minister. A remarkably preserved secret, AUKUS excited a vast and varied reaction in Australia and around the world. The agreement established Morrison as a prime minister of national security and foreign policy consequence. When AUKUS was placed next to the leadership-level Quad, it was likely that decisions on Morrison's watch would shape Australian foreign and security policy for years.

The two principal forces that drove AUKUS were shared alarm at China's military, diplomatic and coercive tactics, and Morrison's initiative to reach out to the United States and United Kingdom with the goal of strengthening Australia's strategic capability. The agreement originated with Morrison. It is another instance of Australia, as junior partner, being the initiator in the Australia–US alliance framework. It sprang from Morrison's statements during 2019 and 2020 that Australia faced its most dangerous strategic outlook since the Second World War.

The five-paragraph statement by the three leaders said the agreement involved 'deeper integration of security and defence-related science, technology, industrial bases and supply chains'. The 'first initiative' was a commitment and 'shared ambition to support Australia in acquiring nuclear-powered submarines' for the Royal Australian Navy. The strategic focus was the Indo-Pacific – as Morrison had envisaged – with Biden saying the future of the world 'depends on a free and open Indo-Pacific'.[221]

The agreement was the trigger for an Australian project of daunting complexity without parallel in our history – the construction of nuclear-powered submarines by a country with no nuclear industry. No country had accomplished this before. Only six nations currently have nuclear-powered submarines – the United States, Russia, China, the United Kingdom, France and India. Australia would join a select group. The challenge goes beyond defence industry. This is a national project that will test to the limit Australia's resources and organisational ability in the naval, industrial, workforce and intellectual domains.

Australia has negligible nuclear industry expertise, no capability in nuclear submarine construction and a navy without nuclear submarine crew skills. From the start, therefore, AUKUS posed a fundamental question: could Australia deliver on the ambition inherent in the agreement and make the transformation required? AUKUS, as it was announced in September 2021, was an in-principle agreement. There was no decision on the design, construction or cost of the nuclear-powered submarines. Everything remained to be decided.

The AUKUS agreement was brought to fruition around two overseas visits made by Morrison in 2021: his attendance in June at the G7 leaders' meeting in the United Kingdom and his visit to the United States in September immediately following the AUKUS announcement.

The meeting Morrison had with Biden at Carbis Bay, Cornwall, in June 2021, which also involved Johnson, is one of the most important held between an Australian prime minister and a US president. This was the first person-to-person Morrison–Biden meeting. It followed the G7 leaders' summit hosted by Johnson, where Morrison, as an invited guest, had briefed the leaders on Beijing's economic coercion and its political demands of Australia.

At the meeting of the three leaders, Morrison proposed to the President for the first time an innovative plan for Australia to access US nuclear power technology to develop its own submarine fleet. The United States had not agreed to this with any nation since 1958 with Britain. Having Johnson present was a critical advantage for Morrison since this was a trilateral concept and Johnson was already committed.[222] The approach to Biden came only after the Morrison–Johnson agreement.

Biden had been briefed by his National Security Advisor, Jake Sullivan, and the US Defense Department had been involved for months. Morrison had been briefed to expect a positive response from Biden, but head-of-government meetings have a life of their own.

Everything hinged on Biden's reaction at this meeting. Without a supportive response from the

President, neither AUKUS nor the submarine deal would materialise. Biden was cautiously positive. It was agreed that more work would be done to bring the idea to fruition. Morrison said there was an 'easy sense' of agreement in the meeting. He praised Johnson as a 'great energiser'. Final US approval was conveyed to Morrison's office only in mid-September, just days before the announcement.[223] This relatively short period suggests an agreement confined to core principles. The next week, Morrison left for New York and Washington, where the agreement was affirmed with the Biden administration and the reaction from Congressional leaders was enthusiastic. Yet the agreement was not signed on this US trip, contrary to Australian expectations.

Amid this Australian–American–British concord, there was embittered dissent from France and President Emmanuel Macron. France's hostility towards Morrison was because Australia had severed its contract with France's Naval Group for the construction of 12 conventionally powered submarines, the biggest defence contract in Australian history. The French were given no prior briefing and were deceived. Given the extreme secrecy surrounding the development of AUKUS, Morrison felt unable to brief the French until the new agreement was finalised. That meant keeping the existing contract operative until the new agreement was in place. But the Prime Minister misjudged the depth of French anger.

Biden also found himself embroiled in blowback from the French, but for different reasons. France was a NATO partner of the United States and United Kingdom. It was a Pacific power with territories, troops and investments in the region. Macron had been pushing for a greater Indo-Pacific role for France, only to find that Biden, behind his back, had cut a far-reaching agreement with Australia at the expense of France's industry, influence and pride. The upshot was that when Morrison travelled to the United States in September, he found a Biden administration keen to lower the symbolism around AUKUS and a president anxious to repair ties with the furious French.

At home, the Labor Party's support for the agreement was decisive. AUKUS needed bipartisanship to endure. Labor's in-principle acceptance of nuclear-powered submarines represented a shift in strategic policy and a turning point in national politics. The extent of change was dramatic. Before this agreement, any notion of bipartisan support for nuclear-powered submarines would have been regarded as inconceivable.[224] Labor leader Anthony Albanese put three conditions on Labor's support:

no development of a civil nuclear power industry; no nuclear weapons; and honouring Australia's obligations under the nuclear non-proliferation treaty. Morrison had already announced the government's adherence to these principles.

The spectre of Australia renewing strategic ties with the United Kingdom and United States ignited fierce and emotional hostility from a number of quarters, including former prime ministers, strategic experts and the Greens. Morrison accentuated this unease with his unwise oversell, branding AUKUS a 'forever partnership' between 'the oldest and most trusted of friends', inviting criticism that Australia had compromised its strategic autonomy in a retreat to an earlier age of dependency. The necessity for secrecy meant neither domestic nor regional opinion had been prepared for the announcement and surprise underpinned the immediate responses, ranging from applause to dismay.

Cancellation of the French deal meant Australia was left with no submarine contract. There was no decision on a new boat, only that there would be at least eight submarines and they would be constructed in Adelaide, a task that many experts felt was beyond Australia.

Morrison announced the formation of a multi-agency taskforce to work with the United States and United Kingdom over 18 months to determine the basis for Australia's nuclear stewardship, calling this a 'forever responsibility'. The taskforce would recommend the specific boat Australia would acquire. Secretary of the Defence Department Greg Moriarty said working groups would be established with the United States and United Kingdom covering design parameters, industrial capability and safety standards.

Speculation revolved around either the British Astute class or American Virginia class nuclear-powered submarines,[225] but there were many questions. Would Australia look at a new design? What was a realistic timeline, given Morrison conceded the initial boats would not be completed until the late 2030s, which many commentators quickly assumed meant 2040? How would Australia fill its submarine capability gap in the intervening period? Would there be a dominant partner and, if so, would it be the United Kingdom or United States? Initial signals were that Morrison was leaning towards the British Astute class with US weapon systems.

Coming after the elevation of the Quad to leaders' level, AUKUS constituted a singular achievement for Morrison's diplomacy. While AUKUS was a surprise, its logic lay in the strategy Morrison had been pursuing since his May 2019 election victory.

AUKUS was no overnight event, but reflected a series of assessments made by Morrison over the preceding two years. Above all, it was a conviction decision and contradicted much of the orthodoxy about Morrison – that he remained a foreign policy practitioner more interested in marketing than strategy. In fact, Morrison possessed a firm strategic sense. The real question about Morrison lay elsewhere: it concerned the wisdom of the strategy that he advanced with such bold moves.

The submarine decision was a direct response to growing strategic competition in the Indo-Pacific, driven by China's military modernisation and aggressive diplomacy. Morrison believed Australia faced a scenario of strategic risk spanning decades, which demanded a far-reaching response. The submarine decision and the associated defence technology arrangements were the most tangible evidence to this point of Morrison's well-enunciated game plan: a deepening of the US alliance within the Indo-Pacific context; greater networks of regional cooperation; and an upgraded defence policy involving higher spending, more offensive capability and an emphasis on high-tech warfare.

To the extent that Beijing saw AUKUS and the Quad as setbacks – and its rhetoric suggested that it did – then its own activities were the driving force.

It is important to grasp that AUKUS is not a treaty or defence compact. There are no formal reciprocal defence obligations. The ANZUS treaty already exists and is being enhanced. Nor is AUKUS a gateway to nuclear weapons. But it does represent a deeper strategic commitment from the three partners. It reinforces existing commitments between the United States and Australia and involves Britain, post-Brexit, in a larger role in the Indo-Pacific. It is obvious that Morrison owes a political debt to Johnson and Biden for their commitments, a guaranteed factor in their future relations.

Biden's authorisation was the crucial event. Morrison felt he could have got Trump to the barrier, but that was now irrelevant. In Biden's first year in the White House, he took decisions of long-run consequence for the alliance in relation to the Quad and AUKUS. This was not because he knew Morrison or was particularly attracted to Australia. It was because Biden, his senior officials and the US system had hardened against China as a strategic rival.

Biden looked to contest China in the Indo-Pacific, a more important signal after his humiliating withdrawal from Afghanistan. This meant Australia was placed in an influential position if it chose to exercise that influence – and Morrison did.

Morrison's instinct that events had given Australia more leverage was vindicated.

Drawing the link between AUKUS and the Quad, Morrison said they were 'complementary', AUKUS being a defence technology agreement while the Quad was a strategic entity designed to contribute to the balance of power in the region.

Biden's decision to change US nuclear policy by extending the technology to another nation had global import. *The Economist* devoted its magazine cover and lead editorial to AUKUS on 25 September, seeing its significance as a 'step towards a new balance of power in the Pacific' with the United States now rebutting Asian fears that America was 'too inconsistent and half-hearted to provide a counterweight' to China.[226] *The Wall Street Journal* editorialised: 'The message to Europe from AUKUS is that the US is serious about resisting Chinese hegemony in the Asia-Pacific . . . Credit to Mr. Morrison for not yielding to China's trade intimidation.'[227]

Lowy Institute Executive Director Michael Fullilove said:

AUKUS is a head-snapping development. The sharing of nuclear secrets between sovereign nations is as intimate as international relations gets. It may not be replicated with other US allies for a long

time, if ever ... Canberra must increase its investment in diplomacy as well as defence – and in new
relationships as well as old ones. For Australia, the
Anglosphere is necessary, but not sufficient.[228]

There was little dispute about the superiority of
nuclear-powered over conventional submarines.
Australian Strategic Policy Institute (ASPI) defence
expert Marcus Hellyer says the nuclear option is
'far better suited to the kinds of operations Australia
conducts in the vast expanses of the Indo-Pacific'.
With 'virtually unlimited energy providing greater
range, endurance and speed, nuclear submarines
will have greater lethality and greater survivability'.
He says the submarines will deliver Australia 'more
strategic weight and show the US and others that as
an ally Australia is carrying its share of the load'.[229]

This analysis aligns with Morrison's thinking.
'We will have to spend more on defence,' Morrison
said at the September 2021 AUKUS launch. He had
argued this for more than a year, but the nuclear
submarine decision brought the point home. 'That's
what the new era looks like,' he said. Morrison noted
that defence spending was running at about 2.2 per
cent of GDP, but declined to put a benchmark on
future spending. Shadow Foreign Minister Penny
Wong said an increase in the defence budget had

'bipartisan support'.[230] It is not possible to put any reliable estimates on the cost of the new submarine program, but the government said it will exceed that of the French contract. Defence spending may grow to three per cent or even higher, but no senior politician is prepared to say that.[231] The management of an increased defence budget, its priorities and the inevitable trade-offs will pose daunting challenges for future governments.

The starting point for AUKUS came in late 2019 when Morrison posed a question that had hung in the background during the Abbott and Turnbull governments: were nuclear-powered submarines an option for Australia? After leaving office, Tony Abbott told the author his greatest mistake as prime minister was his failure to insist on a nuclear-powered submarine for Australia.[232] When the Turnbull government decided in 2016 on the French bid for the conventional submarine contract, the nuclear option was not available. Turnbull was told a civil nuclear industry would be required and beyond that, there was no suggestion that the United States would offer nuclear-powered submarine technology. Turnbull, however, said that before he was removed as Prime Minister, he had 'started to investigate the question again' and felt 'this is a debate that will continue'. In his memoirs, he said having a contract with the French offered a 'potential option' to move to a nuclear design with them.[233]

Morrison asked his defence adviser: should I even ask the question? The answer came back: yes, you should. Morrison took informal soundings. In 2020, a team was established in Defence under Greg Moriarty to assess the nuclear submarine issue, reporting to Morrison and Defence Minister Linda Reynolds. Its conclusion in early 2021 was that the idea was technically possible. The breakthrough was that a civil nuclear industry was not a necessary condition. This was a pivotal change in advice in just three years. Morrison was told that the next generation submarines from the United States and United Kingdom would not need refuelling because the reactors would operate for the life of the boat.

This was the game changer. Australia's allergic hostility to nuclear power had been an ingrained aspect of politics for decades. Morrison had no interest in contesting this prejudice. 'I doubt we could have proceeded if we had to create a civil nuclear industry,' he told colleagues. Having been told this obstacle could be avoided, a pathway emerged.

The next decision was whether Australia should take this issue to the political level. There were several factors at work. Continual problems with

French company Naval Group over costs, delays and difficulties with local contractors had undermined confidence in the existing contract. But Morrison was fixated on an iron rule: don't walk away from the French contract unless there is a Plan B. He was now investigating a Plan B.

Like Abbott and Turnbull before him, Morrison was attracted to the nuclear option. But Morrison wanted to go to Australia's traditional partners, the United States and United Kingdom, not France. He correctly saw nuclear-powered submarines as an issue of the deepest strategic intimacy. Morrison also wanted an approach that gave Australia options with both the United States and United Kingdom – in short, a trilateral compact. But maximising his options this way had a cost – Australia was losing years by restarting the entire process.

Morrison, however, wanted something else: a wider agreement that went beyond just submarines to give Australia access to broader levels of US defence technology. He did not want project-by-project decisions, but an arrangement that plugged Australia more deeply into the US system.

Morrison judged that the United States would be ready to concede Australia such access because of the changed strategic outlook, notably China's behaviour. Morrison also judged that perceptions of Australia had reached another periodic high within the US system – it was seen not just as a reliable ally, but as displaying the courage to defy China's coercion, hence the early statements of support from Biden's aides Jake Sullivan and Kurt Campbell. 'The Americans recognise what we have done,' Morrison told his ministers. 'They know what I have said in the regional and global forums. We have walked the walk. The US knows we are a serious partner.'

When Morrison pressed the button and went to the political level, Australia's dialogue with Sullivan and Campbell was decisive. They backed Australia with Biden and within the US system and were pivotal to securing AUKUS. Between the Carbis Bay meeting in June and the September announcement, there was a huge amount of secret work done in the Australian system (mostly at night, given the time zones in the three jurisdictions), negotiating the terms of the agreement to ensure all of Biden's concerns were addressed.

Australia's dialogue with the United States involved the US Department of Defense, the National Security Agency, military commands, naval officials and Biden's close strategic advisers. Unsurprisingly, there were sceptics in the US system about providing the technology to a non-nuclear power state.

In parallel, Morrison and Defence Minister Peter Dutton, appointed in 2021, strove to lift the tempo of US defence cooperation with Australia through deeper defence technology access. Tied to the AUKUS announcement, Morrison unveiled a series of long-range strike capability acquisitions including Tomahawk cruise missiles to be fielded on Australian destroyers, Joint Air-to-Surface Standoff Missiles for the air force, Long Range Anti-Ship Missiles, precision strike missiles for our land forces and progress with the United States towards a $1 billion guided weapons manufacturing project that would see Australia develop its own missile manufacturing capability. After the September 2021 AUSMIN meeting, Dutton outlined proposals for greater defence force interoperability, expanded access and presence of US forces in Australia and more cooperation in science, technology and logistics.

However, the government plunged into heroic and surely unsustainable territory in announcing that the nuclear-powered submarines would be built in South Australia, thereby 'maximising the use of Australian workers' and ensuring 'a strong and effective sustainment industry'. This revealed the extent to which AUKUS was designed to cover every political need, in particular domestic shipbuilding. Local construction in Adelaide was the core political condition of the previous submarine program, forced upon Abbott in 2015 and entrenched by Turnbull in 2016. It was now to be carried over to the far more daunting nuclear submarine program. This loomed as a serious mistake.

For years, local construction has been driven by Liberal political needs, with South Australian cross-party electoral demands only intensifying over the last decade. This was despite the known consequences: higher costs and longer delays. The language Turnbull used when announcing the French contract in Adelaide in 2016 highlighted the political imperative: 'The submarine project alone will see Australian workers building Australian submarines with Australian steel, here where we stand today, for decades into the future.'[234] Morrison now pledged that South Australia would be a 'hub' for Australia's naval shipbuilding ambitions.

Former secretary of the Defence Department Dennis Richardson, a supporter of AUKUS, warns the local construction policy must be modified: 'It will be essential that the government does not allow domestic political considerations to compromise what will be a national enterprise. In terms of both cost and schedule, it would make sense for the first one or two boats to be substantially built overseas.'[235] There is much informed support for this view.

The debate over local construction, sure to rage for some years, cannot obscure the crucial point: by this decision, Australia will be massively dependent upon the United States and United Kingdom in terms of design, skills, technology and installation. Such technological dependence on the United States is not new. Indeed, it has been integral to Australia's defence posture for decades, but this decision takes dependency into another arena.

Dennis Richardson says:

> This will be the most difficult and complex defence program that this country has ever undertaken by a factor of ten. The first challenge is the absence of trained and skilled personnel in the nuclear submarine area. We have virtually no such high-end skills in Australia. We will need those skills in the actual program to get the thing built. We will need to get a lot of that expertise from the US and UK, but even in those countries those skills are in relatively short supply. We will then need a trained crew. Most of the captains of the US nuclear-powered submarines have PhDs or qualifications in the nuclear area. Again, our navy lacks such expertise.[236]

Turnbull, while saying he wanted AUKUS to be a 'great success', was sceptical of the advice that a civil nuclear industry was not required. 'It sounds too good to be true.' He points out that the advice to him had been the opposite, and that if something goes wrong with a nuclear-powered submarine, the United States and United Kingdom have nuclear facilities and expertise to deal with it. Australia does not. But Turnbull says Australia cannot accept any arrangement to have nuclear submarine maintenance in another country, since that would deny sovereign control.[237]

The background briefing from the White House confirmed the historic nature of the agreement. Senior administration officials said the decision was about the 'new architecture' of defence cooperation in the twenty-first century Indo-Pacific. 'I just want to underscore that this is a fundamental decision – fundamental – that binds decisively Australia to the United States and Great Britain for generations,' a US official said. 'This is the biggest strategic step that Australia has taken in generations.'

In their briefing, US officials said nuclear submarine technology was 'extremely sensitive' and the Biden administration viewed the decision as a 'one-off'. They said the message the President was sending from the United States was 'a deeper sustained commitment to the Indo-Pacific'.[238]

The pivotal question, however, remains: exactly how far does the US commitment on nuclear-powered technology extend? There was no initial answer, given the delay in releasing the agreement. A senior Australian official said:

> We must ensure that over the 18-month review process, Australia can satisfy the US system that we can meet requirements for safety and security to an equivalent standard of the US system itself. This will be the only basis on which the Americans provide the technology to Australia.

For the United States, such requirements are an imperative. Former US secretary of the Navy Don Winter, a leader in the US defence industry with a doctorate in physics, used to tell senior Australians that American engineers engaged in submarine construction were required to listen to the tapes of the agonising final moments of US sailors on board the nuclear submarine USS *Thresher* as its steel buckled and the vessel broke up in an accident in 1963, resulting in the loss of all crew.

The most intense critique of AUKUS, however, centres on the submarine capability gap out to 2040 and extending to 2050. Defence had been predicting that the first Attack class submarine under the French contract would be operational in 2034. With that contract cancelled and the delivery timetable for the nuclear-powered submarines projected in the late 2030s or 2040, this constitutes a further significant delay.

The government had previously decided that all six of the ageing Collins class conventional submarines would undergo major upgrades from 2026 to keep them operative until the late 2030s and beyond.

Will the rebuilt Collins meet the capability gap? There are serious doubts, given there is no margin for error between the expiry of the rebuilt Collins and the planned rollout of the nuclear-powered submarines. The risk is that the Collins boats age faster than the nuclear submarines arrive, with the prospect of the submarine fleet being severely depleted, reduced to only four boats around 2046 and not reaching eight boats until the end of the 2050s.[239]

Against this backdrop, and warnings that the danger from China might escalate in the 2020s, the government faces strong pressure to secure a nuclear-powered submarine capability within the decade. This is easier said than done. Within days of the AUKUS announcement, Peter Dutton said the government would consider leasing or acquiring nuclear submarines in the interim period. He said this would be canvassed with both the United States and United Kingdom. But leasing from either country is extremely difficult and is unlikely to be feasible. Dutton also said it was not 'correct' to think that a nuclear-powered submarine could be purchased 'off the shelf'.[240] Defence Department head Greg Moriarty told a parliamentary committee that Defence had not given any advice to government on an interim submarine capability beyond upgrading the Collins. Early signs are that Morrison is interested in the notion of increased deployments of visiting British nuclear submarines.

The AUKUS agreement, therefore, highlights a serious capability problem for Australia's submarine fleet. It has been obvious for a decade that Australia would not have a new submarine to replace the existing Collins class. It is also folly to think leasing US nuclear submarines, even if possible, is a short-term proposition. It would require legislative frameworks, new port facilities in Australia to manage the boats and supporting skilled personnel on shore. At this stage, it is not apparent what solution might be found to the capability gap.

Announcing the AUKUS agreement on 16 September, Morrison called it 'the single greatest initiative' to advance the national interest and regional stability since the ANZUS alliance was inaugurated 70 years earlier. He said it took the ANZUS treaty 'to a whole new level' and was to the benefit of everybody in the Indo-Pacific with 'no exceptions'.

He praised Johnson and Biden as 'two great friends of freedom and Australia'. Morrison gave a solemn promise that this was not a step towards a nuclear weapons capability, saying there were 'no plans for it, no policy for it, no contemplation of it'. The night before the announcement, he spoke to India's Modi and Japan's Suga. Having tried unsuccessfully to phone Macron, he informed the French president by text – hardly a satisfactory communication.[241]

Four days after the announcement, Morrison left for New York and Washington for a meeting with Biden, meetings with senior officials and the first Quad meeting of the four leaders face-to-face. Morrison emerged with a powerful bipartisan endorsement of the AUKUS agreement from the administration and from Congressional leaders during a day on Capitol Hill. Measured by outcomes, this was a far more significant visit than Morrison's lavish welcome two years earlier from Trump.

Morrison said later that his meetings on Capitol Hill were 'decisive' given that Congress at some later date will need to pass legislation to implement AUKUS. In a euphoric remark after his meetings, Morrison said, 'President Biden gets it, the Congress gets it, the Senate gets it. And that is a great encouragement to Australia. They understand the challenge we've been facing.'[242]

Questioned about conflict with China, Morrison said, 'I am confident that we can avoid the conflict that we all want to avoid, and I believe that includes not only Australia and many countries in our region and friends across ASEAN, but I believe that extends to our partners in the Quad – Japan and India.'[243]

While Morrison's US visit was successful, a large element of the media coverage focused on France's anger. This became an international event with reports that Macron felt betrayed. Heightening the pressure, French Foreign Minister Jean-Yves Le Drian said, 'It's really a stab in the back. We had established a relationship of trust with Australia. This trust has been betrayed.' France recalled its ambassadors from Canberra and Washington.

At home, Turnbull launched an assault:

He [Morrison] deliberately deceived France. This betrayal of trust will dog our relations with Europe for years. The Australian government has treated the French Republic with contempt. It won't be forgotten. Every time we seek to persuade another nation to trust us, somebody will be saying, 'Remember what they did to Macron.'[244]

France was shocked that Biden kept it in the dark while negotiating a new partnership covering the

Indo-Pacific and nuclear-powered submarines. The US system was caught by surprise – Australia had been left to deal with the French, given it had charge of the contract cancellation. But Australia, the United States and United Kingdom had an agreement that the French would not be informed of the cancellation of the contract until the AUKUS announcement was being made. Biden, like Morrison, misjudged the depth of French anger.

The Morrison–Macron relationship had been amicable, perhaps too amicable. They had embraced in Paris in June and dined together just after the Carbis Bay meeting. Morrison told Macron that strategic circumstances had changed since 2016 and that a conventional submarine was now unlikely to meet Australia's needs. But he did not inform the French leader of the AUKUS proposal or say or imply that the existing French contract would be cancelled.

Acknowledging a 'difficult and disappointing' decision for France, Morrison said it in no way reflected upon the French submarine, Naval Group or the French government's commitment to the project. 'As a prime minister I must make decisions that are in Australia's national security interests,' he said. Australia to that stage had invested $2.4 billion in the Attack class program.

Morrison faced intense criticism for diplomatic ineptitude and not providing an earlier briefing to the French. But given Morrison's decision to go with the United States and United Kingdom, there was no exit without trauma. AUKUS was the most secret arrangement an Australian government had entered for half a century. Morrison felt briefing the French would have been untenable, a judgment verified by their subsequent reaction. He tried to ring Macron on the eve of the announcement but Macron, presumably fearing the worst, declined to take the call. The French president sent a text message: 'Should I expect good or bad news for our joint submarine ambitions?' Morrison then forwarded by text a letter informing Macron of the cancelled contract.

Damage to the French relationship will be deeper and last longer than the government anticipated. This became apparent during the subsequent G20 meeting in Rome when Macron, interviewed by Australian journalists, accused Morrison of lying to him. This made the rift personal and played into domestic politics. Facing an attack on his integrity, Morrison hit back, denying the accusation. The government leaked Macron's text message, further inflaming the French. France, like China, insisted that it was Australia's responsibility to repair the relationship. While Morrison had been provoked, the spat revealed the flaws in his personal diplomacy – an emotional overreaction and poor judgment in leaking a personal text from another leader.

While Labor endorsed the agreement, Penny Wong raised a series of critical questions ultimately under the heading of sovereignty. Wong asked, 'With a higher level of technological dependence on the US, how does the Morrison–Joyce government assure Australians that we can act alone when need be; that we have the autonomy to defend ourselves, however and whenever we need to?' Drawing a link between interoperability and loss of operational sovereignty, Wong asked, 'How will we control the use of technology and capability that is not ours?'[245]

The sovereignty argument had been made earlier by Paul Keating, who attacked both the government and Labor. Keating said AUKUS meant 'a lock-in of our military forces with those of the US, with only one underlying objective: the ability to act collectively in any military engagement by the US against China.' Keating said the consequence would be to 'rob Australia of freedom or choice in any engagement it may deem appropriate'.[246]

Liberal and Labor governments for decades have relied on state-of-art technology from allies, principally but not exclusively the United States, to enhance the Australian Defence Force (ADF).

Labor MP Peter Khalil, a former national security adviser to Kevin Rudd as prime minister, wrote a rebuttal of the Keating argument. 'This misunderstands interoperability. We buy equipment from all over the world, but this does not reduce our sovereignty. Interoperability allows our equipment to work with that of our allies. It does not tie us to their operational command.'[247]

Former secretary of Defence Dennis Richardson says:

> When we have these nuclear-powered submarines, they will be under Australian command and control as is the rest of the ADF. We will make our sovereign decisions about what capability we deploy or don't deploy in any conflict. In acquiring nuclear-powered submarines, we are no more dependent on US technology than when we acquired the Joint Strike Fighter from the US. In that sense, the submarines do not constitute any historic break with the past. At no stage in our history have we possessed independent defence industry capability. Therefore, we will always be dependent upon technology from other countries. The submarine is consistent with that history.[248]

The AUKUS agreement brought to a high tide Morrison's strategic ambition of aligning more closely with the United States in the Indo-Pacific and brought to a zenith the criticism that this was the wrong call for Australia. The debate, sure to be intense and long-lasting, is also to be welcomed.

Hugh White says, 'Australia is going along with America in its military confrontation with China' and warns that if war comes, the United States 'will face a failure as complete as its failures in the War on Terror but far, far more devastating'.[249] Paul Keating says AUKUS 'amounts to a massive bet on the United States and its staying power in Asia' and that the Morrison government is 'pushing Australia towards a headlong confrontation with China'. Keating sees the alignment with the United States and United Kingdom as evidence that Australia was turning its back on Asia, finding our security *in* Asia and not *from* Asia.[250]

Peter Varghese supports AUKUS, but says it is more of a technological leap than a 'fundamental strategic departure'. Assessing the US alliance as a 'significant net benefit' for Australia, Varghese issues two warnings. First, while Australia is prudent to prepare for a Cold War involving China, this is the precise outcome it needs to avoid – a new Cold War is neither 'inevitable nor desirable' and would damage Australia's economic and security interests. Second, there are no 'forever' friends and no guarantees from alliance partners, which means Australia must confront the hard decisions and acquire the capability to defend itself.[251]

The AUKUS agreement verified what had been obvious for some time – that Morrison had long since forsaken any sense of strategic ambiguity and was working to buttress Australia's long-run security in relation to China. But this does not deny the enduring duality of Australia's position: our main security partner is America, and our main economic partner is China. In terms of the regional impact of AUKUS, former foreign minister Gareth Evans said, 'Nor, properly understood and implemented, is there anything in the agreement that should generate enduring hostility or anxiety from any other player in the region.'[252]

Morrison's presentation of the agreement, however, was more effective in political terms than in strategic terms. He was not just unapologetic, but proud of the deeper ties with Australia's great and powerful friends. Indeed, he invoked cultural sentimentality, saying, 'At its heart, today's announcements are about the oldest of friendships, the strongest of values and the deepest of commitments. That's what it takes to have a forever partnership.'

His critics say this is a return to the Anglosphere, but Morrison sees no contradiction between the closer security alignment with AUKUS partners and closer strategic ties in the Indo-Pacific. His entire strategy is framed on the assumption that Australia can advance in both domains simultaneously.

Asked about his critics, Morrison said he preferred to be 'in the company of John Curtin and Robert Menzies' on the issue.[253] He expects public support for the initiative will be strong. But with AUKUS, everything lies ahead. Final judgments will depend on the submarine design, the quality of the partnership, the construction program, Australia's response to the technological challenge and the framing of our diplomacy. The road ahead will be filled with obstacles.

Morrison needs a confidence-building strategy around AUKUS. This means more exposition from the Prime Minister about its meaning and direction. Given that Biden was prepared to restore relations with France partly at Australia's expense – by criticising the way AUKUS was presented – it is vital that the Biden administration signals its commitment to the letter and spirit of the agreement. Final assessments of Morrison's strategic judgment and his foreign policy will pivot around implementation of the agreement.

CHAPTER NINE

The Morrison Doctrine

After three years in office and facing a global pandemic, economic coercion from China and a world in disruption, Scott Morrison was shifting the contours of Australian foreign policy – a project as inevitable as it was hazardous.[254]

Morrison relied on traditional norms and faiths in reshaping Australian policy. Some of his moves were bold, but they followed an established strategic outlook. His China policy constituted a sharp departure from that of John Howard, moving the Liberal Party away from Howard's formula of 'not having to choose' between the United States and China. Yet this was widely interpreted within Coalition politics – and much of the media – as being a reaction driven by a different and more dangerous China. Morrison was seen not as staging a revolt against orthodoxy, but as the exponent of a new orthodoxy.

Morrison brings his own style to the conduct of foreign policy. His instinct is for ambition and activism. He listens to experts, but is not necessarily swayed by them. Like most prime ministers, he backs his own views and judgments. He rarely defers to others and puts the stamp of his style, beliefs and judgments all over Australian foreign policy. Anybody who thought Morrison's initial lack of experience might produce a reticent prime minister in the diplomatic domain was soon disabused. He is an enthusiast, but constantly oversells his initiatives. Morrison is a quick learner and, as a politician, has an instinct for power. And he is bold – his secret and sustained effort to secure the nuclear-powered submarine decision is a singular example of executive decision-making that only prime ministers can pull off.

But Morrison's diplomacy got him into recurring trouble. It began with the Jerusalem embassy issue, continued with the call for the pandemic inquiry and reappeared in his insult to the French over cancelling the submarine contract. The government, plagued by the conflict between a fossil fuel economy and the need to reduce emissions, faced continuous international criticism over its climate change diplomacy, criticism that would not be assuaged by the formal commitment to net zero by 2050.

Clear lines of continuity and consistency run through Morrison's speeches, based on his beliefs in sovereignty, agency and liberal democracy. These beliefs have been hammered into policy under the influence of China's coercion against Australia. Morrison's reaction has been intense and grounded in two instincts: that China must be met in strategic terms by a new balance of power, and that the Communist Party's authoritarianism has infected its stance on nearly everything.

The ultimate judgment on Morrison's policy will take years, but if one searches for an encompassing theme, then Morrison himself volunteers this: 'Our interests are inextricably linked . . . to a strategic balance in the region that favours freedom and allows us to be who we are: a vibrant liberal democracy, an outward-looking open economy, a free people determined to shape our own destiny.'[255]

During an interview, Morrison acknowledged the American origins of this theme, sourcing it to Bush administration US national security adviser Condoleezza Rice. In 2002, Rice delivered the Wriston Lecture in New York under the title 'A Balance of Power that Favours Freedom'.

Identifying the great debate in foreign policy literature between the 'realist' and 'idealist' schools, Rice said that in real life 'power and values are married completely' – if the Soviet Union had won the Cold War, then global values would be far different. The aspiration, Rice said, was to 'create a balance of power that favours freedom', a plan subsequently lost in the follies of the Iraq war.[256]

Morrison, however, endorses Rice on this principle. He embraces the concept, but translated to a different time and situation. Asked if this notion – 'a strategic balance that favours freedom' – could be labelled the Morrison Doctrine, he said 'yes' and added, 'If you like, you can be the first to coin it that way.'[257]

Its durability remains to be tested. As argued in this Paper, Australia cannot compete in Southeast Asia just on democratic values. What counts are tangible benefits. ASEAN nations do not want outsiders telling them how to organise their societies. Alert to this, Marise Payne emphasises that Australia's approach is 'inclusive', saying Australia does not exclude countries 'simply because they have a different system from ours' – a point Morrison endorses.[258]

The fusion of power and values has wound its way through all of Morrison's foreign policy remarks. By 2021, Morrison and Payne were articulating five principles that shaped Australian foreign policy.[259] The first was support for open economies and open societies, a values-based stance tied to a rules-based international liberal order. This was a Liberal Party position dedicated to multilateralism, at some remove from the rhetoric of the Howard era and the initial Morrison mindset about 'negative globalism'.

Much of its foundation (though this point would not be conceded by Morrison) lay in the retreat of the United States from its previous global leadership and its lurch to 'America First' introspection, giving China an opening to reset global norms. Morrison's fear is that the more 'the jungle grows back', the more middle-sized nations such as Australia are endangered. 'Competition does not have to lead to conflict,' he says. 'Nor does competition justify coercion.' The task is for liberal democracies to defend the values of free and pluralistic societies.[260]

The second principle enunciated by Morrison and Payne was a focus on building sovereign capacity and resilience. This is a core Morrison conviction on how Australia must evolve and on how the Indo-Pacific must secure its future. It has become a point of intersection between external and domestic policy. Securing our sovereignty by a use of hard and soft power is elemental in Morrison's view of Australia's future.

It was the combined impact of China and COVID-19 that drove Morrison and Treasurer Josh Frydenberg towards economic resilience. They see it as necessary to combat China's trade campaign and essential to buttress self-sufficiency against global pandemics. For Morrison and Frydenberg, this means economic and security policy at home overlap more than before – a significant shift from past governments. This sentiment began to run across a whole-of-government approach typified by trade diversification, protection of critical infrastructure, greater domestic production of everything from vaccines to missiles, energy security, recasting foreign investment with a security priority, and stronger protections against cyber and foreign interference. How the tension between greater resilience and support for pro-market liberalism plays out will be resolved in future years.

Morrison would endorse the remark of Richard Maude that:

> Australia will have little choice but to keep hardening itself domestically, implementing policies that eliminate or minimise the sovereignty and security risks that come with many Chinese Communist Party actions and behaviours, while seeking to promote a balance favourable to our interests in the Indo-Pacific.[261]

The third Morrison–Payne point was working with partners on global strategic challenges. This meant strength in numbers and coalitions. It meant an increase in the defence budget, deeper defence integration with the United States and an expansive vision of ANZUS. It meant the development of the Quad. But the example par excellence for Morrison was the Pacific Step-up that turned Australia's metropolitan responsibilities into a priority. It meant working with Japan and India and engaging ASEAN. Payne put an emphasis on the upgrading of bilateral relations with a number of ASEAN nations, and in October 2021, at the first annual ASEAN–Australia leaders' summit, the relationship was upgraded to a comprehensive strategic partnership.

Morrison is enthusiastic about salvaging the liberal free trade system, and by 2021 he had shifted a long way on global climate change action with his net zero 2050 pledge, aligning with the global benchmark, though this was undercut by his refusal to offer more ambitious medium-term targets for 2030. Morrison continued to push hard to achieve better international cooperation on pandemics. His conclusion from 2020 was that China had an alarming grip on the WHO, and that there was a need to ensure that the organisation and other global bodies were defended against Chinese colonisation.

He backed reform of the WHO to provide for 'enhanced surveillance and pandemic response powers' and supported Biden's demand for greater efforts to identify the origins of COVID-19.[262]

The government had learnt the hard way that COVID-19 exposed the failure of the international order, that vaccine nationalism had consequences, and that US–China rivalry had destroyed any prospect for effective international cooperation against the virus. Morrison had a vested interest in defending his government's demand for an inquiry into the virus. A year later, the extent of China's deception and refusal to cooperate over investigation into the origins of the pandemic gave extra validity to Australia's stance, if not the diplomacy that accompanied it.

Fourth, Morrison and Payne called for a global economic recovery based on markets and business-led growth, repudiating what they saw as the essentially Keynesian social democratic push across Europe and Biden's America for a 'government-centred and government-dependent' recovery. Morrison saw this as a potentially colossal global blunder – a faulty diagnosis – and said this is 'certainly not the Australian way'.

This stance got little attention, but represented a potentially significant point of tension between Australia and transatlantic sentiment. Morrison was up-front: he said the world recession was caused by the pandemic, not by failed economic liberalism. It underlined what Morrison and Frydenberg had argued at home: that the unprecedented levels of financial support during the crisis must not be extended into the recovery or represent an enduring shift in macroeconomic policy.[263]

Fifth and finally, Morrison and Payne said the goal must be 'to demonstrate that liberal democracies work'. Morrison saw this task as both a domestic challenge for democratic liberalism across the West – most exemplified by America's traumas – and also as being basic to the contest of governing systems, given China's argument that its model delivered superior results and that Western democracies were in decay.

Inevitably, this stance raises questions and contradictions. Improved multilateralism has to involve China, from reform of the WTO to climate change to pandemic improvements. How does this fit with Morrison's liberal-democratic schema? On what basis will Australia work with China in these endeavours? Morrison has no answer to these questions.

Moreover, the edifice Morrison constructed around freedom and liberal democracy might suit a Biden presidency, but it is untenable under any return to Trump or a Republican pro-Trump president. Another problem is that building a foreign policy around the principle of liberal democracy is a philosophical stance for a great power such as the United States, but not part of the Australian diplomatic tradition, for good reason.

Most roads in Morrison's foreign policy lead back to China. But does Morrison have a China strategy or just a set of convictions? Allan Gyngell says, 'a set of convictions' is not 'an articulated view of policy'. Gyngell says the nation is yet to hear the 'extended response' from Morrison that Australia needs in the transformed world it faces. Activism does not constitute a strategy.

'I think the Prime Minister has strong convictions, but doesn't have a conceptual view of foreign policy,' Gyngell says.

What's absent is any sense of what we want from China. We can be pretty confident that within three years, China is going to be the largest economy in the world. The role that we see China playing is the big open question for Australia because China is not simply going to operate as a responsible stakeholder or play the role we had previously come to expect from it.[264]

Turnbull as prime minister had said Australia wanted 'to see China build a leadership role it desires in a way which strengthens the regional order that has served us so well'. This is a highly desirable outcome. Yet Turnbull took a series of decisions precisely because Australia felt China was undermining rather than strengthening the regional order.

The lesson is that Australia must be willing to work with China in its naturally expanding ambitions, but remain determined to deny China when it seeks to trample over others, including ourselves. It is nice to think Australia should be able to 'fix' its China problem, but the conclusion from the 2017–21 period is that neither side of politics knows how this can be done short of paying a price that Australia is unwilling to pay.

Three questions remain on the table.

First, does Australia have a viable China strategy? Morrison's critics say 'no', but the government rejects this. Certainly, it has a stance, outlined in August 2021 by Foreign Minister Payne:

In working with China, we seek a relationship that serves the interests of both countries in which each respects the other's interests ... Our relationship with China will continue to be based on four key principles: a commitment to open markets with trade relationships based on rules; protecting our sovereignty, strengthening our democratic institutions and processes and building resilience to coercion; respect for international law and the peaceful resolution of disputes; supporting a strong and resilient regional architecture.[265]

Perhaps it is more accurate to say Australia has no strategy to repair the relationship. The bigger point is that a politically acceptable strategy may not exist. The likelihood is a permanently damaged Australia–China relationship, driven by structural forces and competing interests. If there is no further deterioration, the Morrison government would probably accept that. It would buy time for Australia to adjust as best it can.

Government advisers concede the situation might deteriorate further. In the words of Frances Adamson, China 'is still dogged by insecurity as much as driven by ambition'.[266] Might China respond to the apparent futility of its tactics? If the aim is to intimidate Australia, the project has been a singular failure.

While pessimistic about the immediate future of Australia–China relations, Linda Jakobson says, 'A bilateral relationship does not function in isolation. It will function in a region where Australia needs a working relationship with China. Much will depend on the future course of US–China ties. But there is always the possibility of emergence from a fraught relationship.'[267]

The second question is: did Australia ever assess properly the damage to the relationship from its China reset?

Opinions on this question vary. Ministers and officials are reluctant to concede oversights. Commenting on the NSC, Peter Varghese says, 'The way the NSC works, it takes decisions on individual issues. Governments don't take the temperature at every point.'[268] But senior ministers were told the consequences of Australia's decisions would be adverse.

Acting director-general of ONA in 2017 Bruce Miller says:

The Australian system, including ministers, knew that we would pay a price for our decisions on China. I'm confident the government considered the full range of possible Chinese responses. But it's also probably true China's actions have been toward the upper end of that range. I don't believe we should blame ourselves except at the margin. China has had good reason to go after us – we are the smallest in the Quad, the most economically dependent on China and we have conditioned the Chinese to think we will respond to their pressure.[269]

Senior DFAT officials said every NSC submission on decisions affecting China had an attachment assessing the possible adverse impact. That would be expected. What is more important, however, is that neither Turnbull nor Morrison would have been dissuaded from their decisions. Both prime ministers made it clear that their security-based decisions were Australian national interest decisions, not driven by US influence.

Insiders say much analysis was done, for example, on the fate of South Korea and Norway when they provoked Beijing's trade retaliation. But analysis only goes so far. The real world is different. To this day, the Australian 'system' cannot be sure what exactly drove Beijing's decision-making.

Policy towards China was tied to the rising national security consciousness, and the drivers behind decisions were the prime ministers, ministerial advisers and the security chiefs. Security and intelligence chiefs – Mike Burgess, Duncan Lewis and Andrew Shearer, appointed as cabinet secretary in 2019 and then in 2020 as director-general of ONI – were highly influential.

Shearer believes China's outlook changed from the time of the Global Financial Crisis and that much of the 'system' had been slow to surrender its emotional commitment to the paradigm of engagement with China. For Shearer, the essential question was not whether Australia properly assessed the likely damage to bilateral relations, but whether Australia fully comprehended the strategic challenge it faced from an aggressive China.

The advice from ONI was that China sought technological superiority over the United States and that the next five to ten years would be decisive in this struggle. It described China's tactics as seeking influence and dominance within global institutions, and at the regional level seeking to co-opt elites by finance, economic support and bribery. For Shearer, a critical test for Australia's security was whether an antagonistic power could establish a military presence in the immediate region, a danger that had materialised only once before – in the 1940s.

The third question is: what does Morrison's response to the China challenge reveal about him as Prime Minister?

Morrison has sought to keep open the door with China while engaging in a substantial resilience strategy to ensure Australia can withstand Beijing's pressure. He sees China's tactics as an exercise in intimidation to break Australia and to break him as Prime Minister. Morrison believes that submitting to China will create a template of submission en route to an ultimate relegation to client state status. He is convinced that if Australia does not stand up now, it will face much worse down the track from a weaker position.

He stands by every NSC decision, sure that any sign of weakness will be a mistake. Morrison feels that if China succeeds in dictating to Australia, then it will pocket such success and repeat the tactic. He feels the challenge Australia faces today will be the challenge other nations face tomorrow.

Crucial to Morrison's resistance is domestic political support. It is a rare prime minister who takes a significant foreign policy stance at the cost of public opinion. Morrison has had backing from his cabinet, the coalition parties and a majority of the public. The Labor Party has endorsed every major decision on China, while criticising Morrison's diplomacy and his motives.

Morrison has been assisted by China's ineptitude. Peter Varghese says:

> I think China is probably surprised that we didn't give in, given the sheer extent of the retaliation. Australia has taken the hit. But China's tactics have turned public opinion against Beijing. This gave Scott Morrison political cover when the government, otherwise, would have had to carry more of the blame.[270]

Invited to the G7 meeting in Cornwall in 2021, Morrison told world leaders Australia had been targeted because it dared stand up to China. Morrison's response was engagement – to show Australia could muster strength in numbers, in cooperation with allies, neighbours, democracies and international institutions.

For Morrison, saying that China does not seek to impose its ideology on other nations misses the point. As a great power dealing with others, its tactics are stamped by its governing ideology. Observing China's suppression of Hong Kong's freedom, detention of foreign citizens, rhetorical attacks on Western democracy, human rights abuses, economic coercion and 'wolf warrior' threats, Morrison sees this struggle in moral terms.

Frances Adamson says, 'China may have reached the point where it believes that it can largely set the terms of its future engagement with the world.'[271] Given this situation, Morrison puts a premium on resolve. He says Australia's national character will not be compromised and that 'resolve is so important' in withstanding China's trade retaliation. He sees his response as Prime Minister in the same terms, saying 'if I was to be jittery' that would be exploited with the result being the nation 'would lose confidence'.[272]

Morrison's link between China's coercion and Australian identity is an old idea with deep roots in Australia's history. It was an Australian refrain strong in the immediate post-Federation period when the debate about national security was tied to the perennial question: how does Australia preserve its identity with a small population, unable to defend itself, located on the rim of Asia? The risk in Morrison's emphasis on identity is that he turns a foreign policy issue into an existential one. Such framing must cast a shadow over any prospects for a genuine improvement in relations.

Most of Morrison's remarks about China are restrained. He does not brand China as a direct military threat to Australia. He says Australia does not want economic containment of China. While intensifying Australia's defences, he has not talked up the threat of war. Defence Minister Dutton said that in any Taiwan conflict it is 'inconceivable' that Australia would not support the United States, but Dutton also said that 'nobody wants to see a conflict between China and Taiwan'.[273] On Taiwan, Morrison is careful – Australia does not seek to modify the 'One China' policy. He wants to avoid conflict over Taiwan, given the expectation that Australia would be obliged to support the United States in any military action. The downsides for

Australia in that contingency could be immense and long-term. Payne told the author there was 'no suggestion' of any significant change of policy on Taiwan.[274]

Any US–China war over Taiwan would be devastating for the region and the world. If Australia refused to participate, it would fracture our alliance with the United States. If Australia did participate, war with China would cripple our ties with Beijing for decades. On this issue, Australia, like the region, is largely hostage to calculations involving the United States and China. Australian diplomacy needs to be geared to conflict avoidance.

This is urgent given the rising tensions in 2021 between the United States and China over Taiwan. Admiral Philip Davidson, then head of US Indo-Pacific Command, warned early in the year that China could take military action against Taiwan in the next six years. The United States faces a military challenge in the Western Pacific, where China is increasing its conventional power while also expanding its nuclear arsenal. One objective is to give Beijing the military capability to resolve the Taiwan issue if political means are not forthcoming. The major concern is that President Xi has shortened his timeframe for reunification with Taiwan – a critical factor being China's judgment on whether the option of reunification short of war is receding as Taiwan settles into de facto independence.

The critical issue for Australia is how deeply it becomes integrated into America's diplomatic and military contingencies over Taiwan. This would be a serious step and a significant evolution in alliance cooperation. But the omens are apparent – a 2021 joint ministerial statement said the United States and Australia would strengthen their ties with Taiwan. Any takeover of Taiwan would immeasurably strengthen China's military authority across the region, with grave consequences for Australia. But Australia has no formal security commitment to Taiwan. It needs to avoid, as much as practicable, injecting Taiwan into the already damaged Australia–China relationship. The Taiwan issue has never assumed the salience in Australian domestic thinking that it has long occupied in the United States. It would be an unnecessary mistake for the Morrison government to inject Taiwan into domestic politics during the 2022 election campaign.

The historical analogies Morrison has drawn with the 1930s and the Cold War invite another critique: if this was actually the challenge, then Australia should be doing much more. The temptation is to think Australia might be watching a re-run of an old Liberal Party story – talking up national security and external dangers without taking the tough budgetary and security decisions.

Morrison is alert to this perception. He would endorse the view of one analyst that the China challenge represents a new 'era', not a 'passing moment'.[275] Indeed, his success in securing the AUKUS agreement reflects his effort to think beyond existing norms and put bold strategic initiatives behind the rhetoric.

The ultimate issue is power. At the core of Morrison's foreign policy is his belief that Australia must secure a balance of power across the Indo-Pacific that denies China regional primacy, given it represents an ideology incompatible with Australia's way of life. He champions instead a vision where sovereign states engage freely with each other and where Australia and other nations can function without facing coercion from a hegemonic power.

This is the essence of Morrison's outlook. Judgment on his foreign policy depends, ultimately, on judgments about this vision. Morrison rejects perceptions that China and America are both great powers merely acting the way great powers act. He believes that in terms of national interest and democratic values, Australia's cause is best served by a China that is constrained in its application of power.

So, in meeting the China challenge, Morrison was never going to bet against America.

Dennis Richardson says:

> Whatever the shortcomings of America, we are always going to be closer to the US than to China. That is not just about values, but about national interest. China has shown a propensity to interfere in our domestic affairs. Its retaliatory measures against our trade tell you how China views relations with countries like Australia if you step out of line. In global terms, would Australia be more comfortable with alliances led by the US and like-minded countries or a global framework dominated by China? On every count, the answer is obvious.[276]

Morrison's instinct is almost certainly to think that overreacting to China is the lesser danger than underreacting. He sees China as being on a trajectory of rising nationalism, ideological intensity and strategic assertion. He judges that underestimating this danger is the bigger risk for Australia.

The flaw in Morrison's foreign policy is the absence of working relations with China. Are Australia's relations with China in a state of permanent enmity or can they be resuscitated? The answer will largely depend upon China, but Australia will have a say. Given China's role as the dominant power in East Asia and Australia's major trading partner as far as the eye can see, Australia must look to re-establish functioning relations. There seems no apparent pathway to this goal under Morrison, which suggests this challenge may fall to a future government.

Fundamental to Morrison's outlook is his confidence in America. He sees the risk that America might be a less reliable senior partner because of its domestic fractures, but it is a risk he is prepared to take. Having dealt with Trump, he is fully aware there will always be differences between US and Australian interests in relation to China. A paramount Australian interest lies in avoiding any US–China Cold War or military conflict. But Morrison believes the bigger gamble for Australia lies in hedging its bets – deciding on more accommodation of China and more distancing from the United States. He does not accept that proposition, and feels advocates of this approach take a greater gamble with the nation's security.

The essence of Morrison's response to China is the pursuit of a more resilient Australia, a deeper alignment with the United States and stronger coalitions within the Indo-Pacific. These ideas are not new, but anchored in Australia's contemporary outlook.

In this sense, Morrison's initiatives are built on foundations of deep strategic orthodoxy.

The consistent narrative Morrison has constructed is that Australia must harden itself and develop all-round strengths to succeed in a tougher, more unpredictable, more dangerous world. Morrison himself has been hardened, having to respond to China's assertiveness, a global pandemic, an economic recession and a sharp decline in international cooperation. He consistently talks about greater self-reliance and the need for Australia to do more for itself in economic and strategic terms – being stronger at home to be more effective abroad. This is the direction in which Morrison continues to move. If he becomes the first prime minister since Howard to be re-elected, his mission will be to give that direction more momentum and to persuade the Australian public of its urgency.

Endnotes

1   This ancestral line is on Morrison's mother's side.

2   Scott Morrison, Hansard, House of Representatives, 14 February 2008, 348, https://parlinfo.aph.gov.au/parlInfo/search/display/display.w3p;query=Id%3A%22chamber%2Fhansardr%2F2008-02-14%2F0045%22.

3   Ibid.

4   Scott Morrison, Australia Day National Citizenship Ceremony Speech, 26 January 2019, https://www.youtube.com/watch?v=QPE451X76tQ.

5   Morrison, Hansard, House of Representatives, 14 February 2008.

6   Scott Morrison, interview with the author, April 2021.

7   Morrison, interview with the author, 14 February 2008.

8   Morrison, interview with the author, April 2021.

9   Morrison, Australia Day National Citizenship Ceremony Speech, 26 January 2019.

10 David Goodhart, *The Road to Somewhere: The New Tribes Shaping British Politics*, (London: Hurst & Company, 2017).

11 Morrison, interview with the author, 14 February 2008.

12 Scott Morrison, Lowy Lecture, 3 October 2019, https://www.lowyinstitute.org/publications/2019-lowy-lecture-prime-minister-scott-morrison.

13 Ibid.

14 Scott Morrison, Address – Launch of the 2020 Defence Strategic Update, 1 July 2020, https://www.pm.gov.au/media/address-launch-2020-defence-strategic-update.

15 Paul Kelly, 'Australia's Best Defence is a Good Offence as China Flexes Muscles in Region', *The Weekend Australian*, 4–5 July 2020, https://www.theaustralian.com.au/inquirer/australias-best-defence-is-a-good-offence-as-china-flexes-muscles-in-region/news-story/b73224780eb6c6fa927fa09486ecdbe1.

16 Ibid.

17 Ibid.

18 Scott Morrison, Address, Aspen Security Forum – 'Tomorrow in the Indo-Pacific', 5 August 2020, https://www.pm.gov.au/media/address-aspen-security-forum-tomorrow-indo-pacific.

19 Allan Gyngell, interview with the author, April 2021.

20 Richard Maude, interview with the author, April 2021.

21 Frances Adamson, National Press Club Address, 23 June 2021, https://www.dfat.gov.au/news/speech/national-press-club-address.

22 2017 Foreign Policy White Paper, 'Chapter Two: A Contested World', Australian Government, https://www.dfat.gov.au/sites/default/files/2017-foreign-policy-white-paper.pdf.

23 Scott Morrison, UK Policy Exchange Virtual Address, 23 November 2020, https://www.pm.gov.au/media/uk-policy-exchange-virtual-address.

24 Paul Kelly, 'How We Slayed the Threat of Coronavirus', *The Weekend Australian*, 12–13 December 2020, https://www.theaustralian.com.au/inquirer/how-we-slayed-the-threat-of-coronavirus/news-story/15154f75f89e2b3bedc15 3cb23d2ad2d.

25 Morrison, interview with the author, April 2021.

26 Morrison, Address – Launch of the 2020 Defence Strategic Update, 1 July 2020.

27 Morrison, interview with the author, April 2021.

28 Peter Varghese, interview with the author, April 2021.

29 Morrison, Address, Aspen Security Forum, 2020.

30 Morrison, interview with the author, April 2021.

31 Morrison, Address – Launch of the 2020 Defence Strategic Update, 1 July 2020.

32 Morrison, UK Policy Exchange Virtual Address, 2020.

33 Ibid.

34 Maude, interview with the author, April 2021.

35 Paul Kelly, 'Scott Morrison's Soft-power Diplomacy Triumphs', *The Australian*, 16 March 2021, https://www.theaustralian.com.au/commentary/scott-morrisons-softpower-diplomacy-triumphs/news-story/383b4ecac1396 670306503e464c781dc.

36 Morrison, interview with the author, April, 2021.

37 Ibid.

38 Maude, interview with the author, April 2021.

39   Scott Morrison, 'Raytheon Australia's Centre for Joint Integration – Mawson Lakes, SA', Speech, South Australia, 31 March 2021, https://www.pm.gov.au/media/speech-raytheon-australias-centre-joint-integration-mawson-lakes-sa.

40   Morrison, UK Policy Exchange Virtual Address, 2020.

41   Varghese, interview with the author, April 2021.

42   Richard Maude, 'The Transformation of Australian Foreign Policy', Asia Society, Australia, 27 July 2021, https://asiasociety.org/australia/transformation-australian-foreign-policy.

43   Varghese, interview with the author, May 2021.

44   Alex Oliver, 'A Budget of Skewed Priorities', *The Interpreter*, 7 October 2020, https://www.lowyinstitute.org/the-interpreter/budget-of-skewed-priorities.

45   Michael L'Estrange and Stephen Merchant, *Independent Intelligence Review*, June 2017, https://www.pmc.gov.au/national-security/2017-independent-intelligence-review.

46   Mike Burgess, interview with the author, June 2021.

47   Malcolm Turnbull, interview with the author, June 2021.

48   Malcolm Turnbull, Launch of *Red Zone* at the Lowy Institute, 31 May 2021, https://www.youtube.com/watch?v=sAqew7PEnxQ.

49   Morrison, interview with the author, April 2021.

50   Peter Hartcher, *Red Zone: China's Challenge and Australia's Future* (Carlton, Victoria: Black Inc, 2021), 23.

51   Burgess, interview with the author, June 2021.

52   Ibid.

53   Malcolm Turnbull, *A Bigger Picture*, (Melbourne: Hardie
      Grant, 2000), 435.

54   Josh Frydenberg, Foreign Investment Policy, 5 June
      2020, https://ministers.treasury.gov.au/ministers/josh-
      frydenberg-2018/media-releases/major-reforms-australias-
      foreign-investment-framework.

55   Senate Economics References Committee, *Foreign
      Investment Review Framework*, Interim Report, 4
      February 2016, Chapter 4, https://www.aph.gov.au/
      Parliamentary_Business/Committees/Senate/Economics/
      Foreign_Investment_Review/Interim_Report.

56   Morrison, interview with the author, April 2021.

57   Turnbull, *A Bigger Picture*, 425.

58   Morrison, interview with the author, April 2021; and see
      Peter Hartcher, 'Revealed: Why the Sale of Ausgrid to
      Chinese Buyers was Vetoed', *The Sydney Morning Herald*,
      28 May 2018, https://www.smh.com.au/opinion/revealed-
      why-the-sale-of-ausgrid-to-chinese-buyers-was-vetoed-
      20180528-p4zhxh.html.

59   Morrison, interview with the author, April 2021.

60   Morrison, interview with the author, April 2021.

61   Scott Morrison and Peter Dutton, 'New Conditions on the
      Sale of Australian Electricity Assets to Foreign Investors',
      Joint Statement, Parliament of Australia, 1 February 2018,
      https://parlinfo.aph.gov.au/parlInfo/search/display/display.
      w3p;query=Id:%22media/pressrel/5765806%22.

62   Morrison, interview with the author, September 2021.

63   Malcolm Turnbull, George Brandis and Mathias Cormann,
      Joint Press Conference, 5 December 2017, https://parlinfo.
      aph.gov.au/parlInfo/search/display/display.w3p;query=Id%
      3A%22media%2Fpressrel%2F5676717%22.

64 Malcolm Turnbull, Speech Introducing the National Security Legislation Amendment (Espionage and Foreign Interference) Bill 2017, 7 December 2017, https://www.malcolmturnbull.com.au/media/speech-introducing-the-national-security-legislation-amendment-espionage-an.

65 Burgess, interview with the author, June 2021.

66 Turnbull, interview with the author, June 2021.

67 Burgess, interview with the author, June 2021.

68 Duncan Lewis, interview with the author, October 2020.

69 Morrison, interview with the author, April 2021.

70 Lee Hsien Loong, Press Conference – The Istana, Singapore, 11 June 2021, https://www.pm.gov.au/media/press-conference-istana-singapore.

71 David Crowe, 'Who is This? Australians Can Probably Relate to Angela Merkel's Predicament', *The Sydney Morning Herald*, 2 December 2018, https://www.smh.com.au/politics/federal/who-is-this-australians-can-probably-relate-to-angela-merkel-s-predicament-20181202-p50jqo.html.

72 Morrison, interview with the author, April 2021.

73 Scott Morrison and Julie Bishop, Press Conference with the Minister for Foreign Affairs, 16 October 2018, https://www.pm.gov.au/media/press-conference-minister-foreign-affairs.

74 Penny Wong, ABC Radio National Breakfast, 18 October 2018, https://www.abc.net.au/radionational/programs/breakfast/penny-wong/10389930.

75 John McCarthy, 'A Move to Jerusalem: At What Cost?', *The Strategist*, ASPI, 17 October 2018, https://www.aspistrategist.org.au/a-move-to-jerusalem-at-what-cost/.

76 Scott Morrison, Address to The Sydney Institute,
15 December 2018, https://www.pm.gov.au/media/address-
sydney-institute; and Paul Kelly, 'PM's Israel Fallback
Leaves Australia in an Absurd Situation', *The Australian*,
16 December 2018, https://www.theaustralian.com.au/news/
pms-israel-fallback-leaves-australia-in-an-absurd-situation/
news-story/010bda63c80f965a43d36ba908fca0c0.

77 Dave Sharma, interview with the author, September
2021.

78 Scott Morrison, Address – Australia and the Pacific: A
New Chapter, 8 November 2018, https://www.pm.gov.au/
media/address-australia-and-pacific-new-chapter.

79 Morrison, interview with the author, April 2021.

80 Sharma, interview with the author, September 2021.

81 Alex Hawke, interview with the author, April 2021.

82 Ibid.

83 Jonathan Pryke and Alexandre Dayant, 'China's Declining
Pacific Aid Presence', *The Interpreter*, 30 September 2020,
https://www.lowyinstitute.org/the-interpreter/china-s-
declining-pacific-aid-presence.

84 Morrison, Lowy Lecture, 3 October 2019.

85 Ibid.

86 Marise Payne, 'Australia and the World in the Time of
COVID-19', Speech, National Security College, ANU,
16 June 2020, https://www.foreignminister.gov.au/
minister/marise-payne/speech/australia-and-world-time-
covid-19.

87 Records provided to the author by the Prime Minister's
Office.

88 Morrison, interview with the author, April 2021.

89   Marise Payne, interview with the author, October 2021.

90   Scott Morrison, Keynote Address to Asia Briefing Live –
      The Beliefs that Guide Us, 1 November 2018, https://www.
      pm.gov.au/media/keynote-address-asia-briefing-live-beliefs-
      guide-us.

91   Phillip Coorey, 'Patience and Consistency Key to Ties:
      PM', *The Australian Financial Review*, 31 August 2020,
      https://www.afr.com/politics/federal/patience-and-
      consistency-key-to-ties-pm-20200830-p55qnj.

92   Geoff Raby, La Trobe China University China Studies
      Oration, 29 October 2019, https://www.latrobe.edu.au/
      news/announcements/2019/dr-geoff-raby-presented-the-
      la-trobe-university-2019-china-studies-oration.

93   Adamson, National Press Club Address, 2021.

94   Jennifer Hewett, Michael Smith and Phillip Coorey,
      'China Puts Malcolm Turnbull's Government into the
      Deep Freeze', *The Australian Financial Review*, 11 April
      2018, https://www.afr.com/world/asia/chinas-big-chill-for-
      australia-20180411-h0ymwb.

95   Turnbull, Lowy Institute, 2021.

96   These were outlined in detail in James Laurenceson,
      Michael Zhou and Thomas Pantle, 'Interrogating
      Chinese Economic Coercion: The Australian Experience
      Since 2017', *Security Challenges*, Volume 16, No. 4
      (2020), https://regionalsecurity.org.au/security_challenge/
      1992/.

97   Turnbull, *A Bigger Picture*, 431.

98   Ibid, 430–432.

99   Turnbull, Lowy Institute, 2021.

100   Maude, interview with the author, April 2021.

101 Frances Adamson, 'ANU National Security College 10th Anniversary Lecture Series', ANU National Security College, Canberra, 25 November 2020, https://www.dfat.gov.au/news/speech/anu-national-security-college-10th-anniversary-lecture-series.

102 Varghese, interview with the author, April 2021; and Peter Varghese, 'China Seeks Client States Not Ideological Conquests', *The Australian Financial Review*, 22 June 2021, https://www.afr.com/policy/foreign-affairs/china-s-seeking-client-states-not-ideological-conquests-20210621-p582sg.

103 Mike Pence, Vice President Mike Pence's Remarks on the Administration's Policy towards China, Speech, Hudson Institute, 4 October 2018, https://www.hudson.org/events/1610-vice-president-mike-pence-s-remarks-on-the-administration-s-policy-towards-china102018.

104 Scott Morrison, Address to the Perth USAsia Centre – Perth, WA, 9 June 2021, https://www.pm.gov.au/media/address-perth-usasia-centre-perth-wa.

105 Jacob Greber, 'Frances Adamson: Businesses Need a Plan B for China', *The Australian Financial Review*, 28 May 2021, https://www.afr.com/politics/federal/dfat-boss-businesses-need-a-plan-b-for-china-20210527-p57vuf.

106 Philip Coorey, 'Scott Morrison: 'We Won't Choose' between US, China', *Australian Financial Review*, 16 November 2018, https://www.afr.com/world/asia/scott-morrison-a-turning-point-in-china-ties-20181115-h17y1g.

107 Scott Morrison, Doorstop Singapore, Transcript, 15 November 2018, https://www.pm.gov.au/media/doorstop-singapore; and Coorey, 'Scott Morrison: "We Won't Choose"', *The Australian Financial Review*, 16 November 2018.

108 Turnbull, *A Bigger Picture*, 423.

109 Scott Morrison and Shinzo Abe, Joint Press Statement with His Excellency Shinzo Abe, Prime Minister of Japan, Darwin, 16 November 2018, https://www.pm.gov.au/media/joint-press-statement-his-excellency-shinzo-abe-prime-minister-japan.

110 Varghese, interview with the author, May 2021.

111 Geoff Raby, *China's Grand Strategy and Australia's Future in the New Global Order*, (Melbourne: Melbourne University Press, 2020), 24–28, 130–134 and 154–155.

112 Sharma, interview with the author, September 2021.

113 Scott Morrison, Address to APEC CEO Summit 2018, Port Moresby, PNG, 17 November 2018, https://www.pm.gov.au/media/address-apec-ceo-summit-2018.

114 John Bolton, *The Room Where It Happened*, (New York: Simon & Schuster, 2020), 297.

115 Pence, Hudson Institute, 2018.

116 Scott Morrison, Address to Asialink – 'Where We Live', Bloomberg Q & A, 26 June 2019, https://asialink.unimelb.edu.au/stories/australia-and-the-indo-pacific-an-address-by-prime-minister-scott-morrison.

117 Ibid.

118 Sharma, interview with the author, September 2021.

119 Morrison, Address, Aspen Security Forum, 2020.

120 Lewis, Interview with the author, October 2020.

121 Andrew Tillett, 'Chinese Furious over Australia's Travel Ban "Overreaction"', *The Australian Financial Review*, 14 February 2020, https://www.afr.com/politics/federal/chinese-furious-over-australia-s-travel-ban-overreaction-20200214-p540s1.

122 Payne, interview with the author, October 2021.

123 Richard Ferguson, Elias Visontay and Angelica Snowden, 'Coronavirus Australia Live Updates: Heat Builds on Scott Morrison over $53m WHO Funding', *The Australian*, 15 April, 2020, https://www.theaustralian. com.au/nation/coronavirus-australia-live-updates-donald-trump-hits-back-at-mutinous-governors/news-story/9a0d6c 0added4246131b1f5637c8bf87.

124 Paul Kelly, 'Coronavirus: Trust Rediscovered as PM Resists Pull to Political Extremes', *The Australian*, 2 May 2020, https://www.theaustralian.com.au/inquirer/coronavirus-trust-rediscovered-as-pm-resists-pull-to-political-extremes/ news-story/2f1e82841f440d343d22729b822acb79.

125 Ibid.

126 Samantha Maiden, 'Coronavirus: Peter Dutton 'Demands Answers' of China over Virus Origins', News.com.au, 17 April 2020, https://www.news.com.au/lifestyle/health/ health-problems/coronavirus-peter-dutton-demands-answers-of-china-over-virus-origins/news-story/4c7b86 aa7ce6236a13d193720cd6abb7; and Philip Williams, 'Politicians are Demanding Answers from China about Coronavirus. Some Want to Take Things Further', ABC News, 17 April 2020, https://www.abc.net.au/news/2020-04-17/could-coronavirus-reset-the-way-the-world-interacts-with-china/12158180.

127 'Marise Payne Calls for Global Inquiry into China's Handling of the Coronavirus Outbreak', ABC News, Insiders, 19 April 2020, https://www.abc.net.au/ news/2020-04-19/payne-calls-for-inquiry-china-handling-of-coronavirus-covid-19/12162968.

128 Andrew Tillett, 'China Consumer Backlash Looms over Morrison's Coronavirus Probe', *The Australian Financial Review*, 26 April 2020, https://www.afr.com/politics/ federal/china-consumer-backlash-looms-over-morrison-s-coronavirus-probe-20200423-p54mpl.

129 Paul Karp and Helen Davidson, 'China Bristles at Australia's Call for Investigation into Coronavirus Origin', *The Guardian*, 29 April 2020, https://www.theguardian.com/world/2020/apr/29/australia-defends-plan-to-investigate-china-over-covid-19-outbreak-as-row-deepens.

130 Varghese, interview with the author, April 2021.

131 Hugh White, 'Australia Must Get Better at Picking Its Fights with China', East Asia Forum, 10 May 2020, https://www.eastasiaforum.org/2020/05/10/australia-must-get-better-at-picking-its-fights-with-china/.

132 Payne, interview with the author, October 2021.

133 Morrison, interview with the author, September 2021.

134 Turnbull, Lowy Institute, 2021.

135 Fergus Hanson, Emilia Currey and Tracy Beattie, 'The Chinese Communist Party's Coercive Diplomacy', ASPI, 1 September 2020, https://www.aspi.org.au/report/chinese-communist-partys-coercive-diplomacy.

136 Will Glasgow and Geoff Chambers, 'China a Vindictive and Unreliable Trading Partner: Ambassador Graham Fletcher', *The Australian*, 26 March 2021, https://www.theaustralian.com.au/nation/politics/no-accountability-chinas-fresh-attack-on-australia-over-alleged-war-crimes/news-story/7401f9078ef37c7cefa110f0a9a1c5a4.

137 Roland Rajah, 'The Big Bark but Small Bite of China's Trade Coercion', *The Interpreter*, 8 April 2021, https://www.lowyinstitute.org/the-interpreter/big-bark-small-bite-china-s-trade-coercion.

138 Josh Frydenberg, 'Building Resilience and the Return of Strategic Competition', Speech, ANU Crawford Leadership Forum, Melbourne, 6 September 2021,

https://joshfrydenberg.com.au/wp-content/uploads/2021/09/Treasurer-Speech-Building-Resilience-and-the-Return-of-Strategic-Competition-ANU-Crawford-Leadership-Forum-6-September-2021.pdf.

139 Morrison, interview with the author, April 2021.

140 Paul Kelly, 'China Deal: Sovereignty Rules with the Flex of Constitutional Muscle', *The Australian*, 29 August 2020, https://www.theaustralian.com.au/inquirer/china-deal-sovereignty-rules-with-the-flex-of-constitutional-muscle/news-story/62d74e738265f519b80b236b9b7d115e.

141 Ibid.

142 Scott Morrison and Marise Payne, Press Conference – Australian Parliament House, ACT, Joint Media Statement, 27 August 2020, https://www.pm.gov.au/media/press-conference-australian-parliament-house-act-27aug20.

143 Lowy Institute Poll 2021, https://poll.lowyinstitute.org/.

144 Jonathan Kearsley, Eryk Bagshaw and Anthony Galloway, '"If You Make China the Enemy, China Will be the Enemy": Beijing's Fresh Threat to Australia', *The Sydney Morning Herald*, 18 November 2020, https://www.smh.com.au/world/asia/if-you-make-china-the-enemy-china-will-be-the-enemy-beijing-s-fresh-threat-to-australia-20201118-p56fqs.html.

145 Jonathan Kearsley, 'PM Refuses to Back Down to China over Leaked Dossier of "Grievances"', Nine.com.au, 19 November 2020, https://www.9news.com.au/world/australia-china-trade-relations-morrison-refuses-to-compromise-national-interests/535fb00c-0594-41b3-94e0-0b5494a9cebe.

146 Greg Brown and Rosie Lewis, 'China Talks Only If there are No Conditions, Scott Morrison Says', *The Australian*, 25 January 2021, https://www.theaustralian.com.au/nation/politics/china-talks-only-if-there-are-no-conditions-scott-morrison-says/news-story/5ccc2490da78cc2cee8969aa3284f277.

147 Scott Morrison, Address – National Press Club, Barton, ACT, 1 February 2021, https://www.pm.gov.au/media/address-national-press-club-barton-act.

148 Turnbull, Lowy Institute, 2021.

149 Payne, interview with the author, October 2021.

150 Ibid.

151 Raby, *China's Grand Strategy*, 154–159.

152 Linda Jakobson, interview with the author, October 2021.

153 Hugh White, East Asia Forum, 2020.

154 Gyngell, interview with the author, April 2021.

155 Jakobson, interview with the author, October 2021.

156 Varghese, interview with the author, May 2021.

157 Maude, interview with the author, April 2021.

158 Morrison, interview with the author, April 2021.

159 Maude, interview with the author, April 2021.

160 Turnbull, *A Bigger Picture*, 443–448.

161 Morrison, interview with the author, April 2021.

162 Ibid.

163 Ibid.

164 Simon Benson, 'Morrison Pushes for Asia Deal', *The Australian*, 29 June 2019, https://www.theaustralian.com.au/nation/politics/morrison-pushes-for-asia-deal-as-china-and-us-argue/news-story/4e41cae00bf003750da3bdcbc650457c.

165 Morrison, interview with the author, April 2021.

166 2017 Foreign Policy White Paper, 'Chapter Two: A Contested World'.

167 Morrison, interview with the author, April 2021.

168 Varghese, interview with the author, April 2021.

169 Scott Morrison, 'ANZUS Treaty: 70th Anniversary', Speech, House Debates, 1 September 2021, https://www.openaustralia.org.au/debates/?id=2021-09-01.5.2&s=speaker%3A10081.

170 Morrison, interview with the author, April 2021.

171 Morrison, 'ANZUS Treaty: 70th Anniversary', Speech, 2021.

172 Hugh White, 'Great Expectations: Can Australia Depend on Its Neighbours?', *Australian Foreign Affairs*, Issue 10, October 2020, https://www.australianforeignaffairs.com/articles/extract/2020/10/great-expectations.

173 White, East Asian Forum, 10 May 2021.

174 James Curran, 'ANZUS Nostalgia Exposes Australia's Lack of Strategic Imagination', *The Australian Financial Review*, 29 August 2021, https://www.afr.com/policy/foreign-affairs/anzus-nostalgia-exposes-australia-s-lack-of-strategic-imagination-20210826-p58m3n.

175 Raby, *China's Grand Strategy*, 130.

176 Gyngell, interview with the author, April 2021.

177 Dennis Richardson, interview with the author, October 2021.

178 Morrison, Address to Asialink, 2019.

179 Morrison, interview with the author, April 2021.

180 Hugh White, 'A Very Unreassuring Bombshell: Richard Nixon and the Guam Doctrine, July 1969', *The Strategist*, ASPI, 25 July 2019, https://www.aspistrategist.org.au/a-very-unreassuring-bombshell-richard-nixon-and-the-guam-doctrine-july-1969/.

181 Varghese, interview with the author, April 2021.

182 Scott Morrison, Remarks, Ceremonial Welcome, White House, Washington, DC, 20 September 2019, https://www.pm.gov.au/media/remarks-ceremonial-welcome-white-house-washington-dc.

183 Morrison, interview with the author, April 2021.

184 Morrison, Lowy Lecture, 3 October 2019.

185 Morrison, Address – Launch of the 2020 Defence Strategic Update, 1 July 2020.

186 Brad Norington and Cameron Stewart, 'US Calls for Help Battling China', *The Australian*, 5 August 2019, https://www.theaustralian.com.au/nation/step-up-to-the-plate-on-china-says-pompeo/news-story/f5295e97f7b68ca01b15c53ff01de569.

187 Morrison, Remarks, Ceremonial Welcome, White House, 2019.

188 Scott Morrison, Transcript – Doorstop Interview – Washington, 21 September 2019, https://www.pm.gov.au/media/transcript-doorstop-interview-washington.

189 Scott Morrison, Chicago Council on Global Affairs, Speech, 23 September 2019, https://www.pm.gov.au/media/chicago-council-global-affairs.

190 Morrison, Address to Asialink, 2019.

191 Mike Pompeo, Remarks at the Richard Nixon Presidential Library and Museum, 23 July, 2020, https://www.youtube.com/watch?v=nyXktY0sZGI.

192 Marise Payne, Australia–United States Ministerial Consultations (AUSMIN), Joint Transcript, 29 July 2020, https://www.foreignminister.gov.au/minister/marise-payne/transcript/australia-united-states-ministerial-consultations-ausmin.

193 Varghese, interview with the author, April 2021.

194 Morrison, interview with the author, April 2021.

195 Ibid.

196 Peter Hartcher, '"Just Not Going to Happen": US Warns China over Australian Trade Stoush', *The Sydney Morning Herald*, 16 March 2021, https://www.smh.com.au/world/north-america/just-not-going-to-happen-us-warns-china-over-australian-trade-stoush-20210316-p57b4l.html.

197 Kurt Campbell, A Conversation with Kurt Campbell, White House Coordinator for the Indo-Pacific, Asia Society Policy Institute, 6 July 2021, https://www.youtube.com/watch?v=on5brIIInrI.

198 Jakobson, interview with the author, October 2021.

199 Joe Biden, Remarks by President Biden on America's Place in the World, Speech, 4 February 2021, https://www.whitehouse.gov/briefing-room/speeches-remarks/2021/02/04/remarks-by-president-biden-on-americas-place-in-the-world/.

200 Joe Biden, Inaugural Address by President Joseph R. Biden, Jr, Speech, 20 January, 2021, https://www.whitehouse.gov/briefing-room/speeches-remarks/2021/01/20/inaugural-address-by-president-joseph-r-biden-jr/.

201 Morrison, Address to the Perth USAsia Centre, 2021.

202 Joe Biden, Remarks by President Biden on the End of the War in Afghanistan, Speech, 31 August 2021, https://www.whitehouse.gov/briefing-room/speeches-remarks/2021/08/31/remarks-by-president-biden-on-the-end-of-the-war-in-afghanistan/.

203 Morrison, interview with the author, September 2021.

204 Joe Biden, Remarks by President Biden, Prime Minister Modi of India, Prime Minister Morrison of Australia, and Prime Minister Suga of Japan in the Virtual Quad Leaders' Summit, Speeches, 12 March 2021, https://www.whitehouse.gov/briefing-room/speeches-remarks/2021/03/12/remarks-by-president-biden-prime-minister-modi-of-india-prime-minister-morrison-of-australia-and-prime-minister-suga-of-japan-in-virtual-meeting-of-the-quad/.

205 Morrison, interview with the author, April 2021.

206 Kevin Rudd, 'Why the Quad Alarms China', *Foreign Affairs*, 6 August 2021, https://www.foreignaffairs.com/articles/united-states/2021-08-06/why-quad-alarms-china.

207 Ben Packham, 'Quad Our Biggest Pact in 70 Years, Says Scott Morrison', *The Australian*, 16 March 2021, https://www.theaustralian.com.au/nation/politics/quad-our-biggest-pact-in-70-years-says-scott-morrison/news-story/cddb157756cd79e66dff42104413f0c2.

208 Bruce Miller, interview with the author, June 2021.

209 Varghese, interview with the author, April 2021.

210 Alexander Downer, 'Why the Quad's a Big Strategic Step Forward for Australia', *The Australian Financial Review*, 21 March 2021, https://www.afr.com/policy/foreign-affairs/why-the-quad-s-a-big-strategic-step-forward-for-australia-20210321-p57cl3.

211 Julie Bishop, interview with the author, November 2020.

212 Rory Medcalf, *Contest for the Indo-Pacific: Why China Won't Map the Future*, (Carlton, Victoria: La Trobe University Press/Black Inc, 2020), 4.

213 Morrison, interview with the author, April 2021.

214 Morrison, UK Policy Exchange Virtual Address, 2020.

215 Medcalf, *Contest for the Indo-Pacific*, 7–8.

216 White, *Great Expectations*, 14–24.

217 Paul Kelly, 'Quad Security Dialogue Stepped Up to Leader Level in Response to China', *The Australian*, 10 March 2021, https://www.theaustralian.com.au/commentary/quad-security-dialogue-stepped-up-to-leader-level-in-response-to-china/news-story/f2d0380976fbc29648d9a9854142628d.

218 Scott Morrison, Doorstop Interview – Tokyo, Japan, 17 November 2020, https://www.pm.gov.au/media/doorstop-interview-tokyo-japan.

219 Scott Morrison and Yoshihide Suga, Japan–Australia Leaders' Meeting Joint Statement, 17 November 2020, https://www.pm.gov.au/media/japan-australia-leaders-meeting-joint-statement.

220 Scott Morrison, Address to the 6th Raisina Dialogue, Speech, 15 April 2021, https://www.pm.gov.au/media/address-6th-raisina-dialogue.

221 Scott Morrison, Joe Biden and Boris Johnson, Joint Media Statement, Address: AUKUS – Canberra, ACT, 16 September 2021, https://www.pm.gov.au/media/address-aukus-canberra-act.

222 Ibid.

223 Ibid.

224 Anthony Albanese, Sydney Press Conference Discussing the AUKUS Alliance, National Security and More, 16 September 2021, https://anthonyalbanese.com.au/media-centre/sydney-press-conference-16-sept-2021.

225 Morrison, Biden and Johnson, Address: AUKUS, 2021.

226 'AUKUS Reshapes the Strategic Landscape of the Indo-Pacific', *The Economist*, 25 September 2021, https://www.economist.com/briefing/2021/09/25/aukus-reshapes-the-strategic-landscape-of-the-indo-pacific.

227 The Editorial Board, 'A Smart Submarine Deal with the Aussies', *Wall Street Journal*, 16 September 2021, https://www.wsj.com/articles/a-smart-submarine-deal-for-the-aussies-us-uk-australia-china-france-aukus-11631830017.

228 Michael Fullilove, 'What a New Defence Pact Reveals about America', *The Atlantic*, 21 September, 2021, https://www.theatlantic.com/ideas/archive/2021/09/us-australia-allies/620135/.

229 Marcus Hellyer, 'Australia's Credibility Rests on Subs Success', ASPI, 17 September 2021, https://www.aspi.org.au/opinion/australias-credibility-rests-subs-success.

230 Paul Kelly, 'AUKUS Alliance: Morrison has Seated Australia at Top Table of Diplomacy', *The Weekend Australian*, 25–26 September 2021, https://www.theaustralian.com.au/inquirer/aukus-alliance-morrison-has-seated-australia-at-top-table-of-diplomacy/news-story/966c44a860127207ffbbc75ac3a8e7cb.

231 Peter Jennings, 'AUKUS Sets a Better Direction for Australia's Defence', ASPI, 17 September 2021, https://www.aspistrategist.org.au/aukus-sets-a-better-direction-for-australias-defence/.

232 Tony Abbott, interview with the author, December 2019.

233 Turnbull, *A Bigger Picture*, 343–344.

234 Malcolm Turnbull, Doorstop with Minister for Defence Marise Payne, Minister for Industry Christopher Pyne and Chief of Navy Tim Barrett, Osborne, South Australia, Transcript, 26 April 2016, https://pmtranscripts.pmc.gov.au/release/transcript-40319.

235 Greg Sheridan, 'Problems Stack Up with Confused Nuclear Subs Plan', *The Weekend Australian*, 2–3 October 2021, https://www.theaustralian.com.au/inquirer/plan-to-make-nuclear-subs-locally-is-dead-in-the-water/news-story/521d6a1cc93cf56523a7d9435bba6b1e.

236 Paul Kelly, 'AUKUS Alliance', *The Weekend Australian*, 25–26 September 2021.

237 Malcolm Turnbull, Address to the National Press Club, 29 September 2021, https://www.malcolmturnbull.com.au/media/address-to-the-national-press-club-september-2021.

238 White House Briefing Room, Background Press Call on AUKUS, 16 September 2021, https://www.whitehouse.gov/briefing-room/press-briefings/2021/09/15/background-press-call-on-aukus/.

239 Marcus Hellyer, 'No Room for Delay in Australia's Transition to Nuclear-powered Submarines', ASPI, 27 September 2021, https://www.aspistrategist.org.au/no-room-for-delay-in-australias-transition-to-nuclear-powered-submarines/.

240 Peter Dutton, Interview with Andrew Clennell, Sunday Agenda, Sky News, 20 September 2021, https://www.minister.defence.gov.au/minister/peter-dutton/transcripts/interview-andrew-clennell-sunday-agenda-sky-news.

241 Scott Morrison, Press Conference – Canberra, ACT, 16 September 2021, https://www.pm.gov.au/media/press-conference-canberra-act-24.

242 Scott Morrison, Press Conference, Washington, DC, 22 September, 2021, https://www.youtube.com/watch?v=11c9v5aQX98.

243 Scott Morrison, Press Conference, New York, 21 September 2021, https://www.youtube.com/watch?v=zBpquK-XgMA.

244 Turnbull, Address to the National Press Club, 29 September 2021.

245 Penny Wong, An Address by Senator The Hon Penny Wong to Launch USSC Report 'Correcting the Course', 23 September 2021, https://www.ussc.edu.au/events/an-address-by-senator-the-hon-penny-wong-to-launch-ussc-report-correcting-the-course.

246 Paul Keating, 'This Pact Ties Australia to Any US Military Engagement against China', *The Sydney Morning Herald*, 16 September 2021, https://www.smh.com.au/national/this-pact-ties-australia-to-any-us-military-engagement-against-china-20210916-p58s5k.html.

247 Peter Khalil, 'Why My Hero Keating is Wrong on China and our National Security', *The Sydney Morning Herald*, 23 September 2021, https://www.smh.com.au/politics/federal/why-my-hero-keating-is-wrong-on-china-and-our-national-security-20210922-p58twd.html.

248 Richardson, interview with the author, September 2021.

249 Hugh White, 'War of Error', *The Monthly*, October 2021, https://www.themonthly.com.au/issue/2021/october/1633010400/hugh-white/war-error#mtr.

250 Paul Keating, 'Morrison is Making an Enemy of China – and Labor is Helping Him', *The Sydney Morning Herald*, 22 September 2021, https://www.smh.com.au/world/asia/morrison-is-making-an-enemy-of-china-and-labor-is-helping-him-20210921-p58tek.html; and Paul Keating 'The Morrison Government is Provoking China to Please America', *Australian Financial Review*, 3 September 2021, https://www.afr.com/policy/foreign-affairs/the-morrison-government-is-provoking-china-to-please-america-20210902-p58o9i.

251 Peter Varghese, 'AUKUS is a Good Plan B for China. But Let's Not Bring on Cold War 2.0', *The Australian Financial Review*, 21 September 2021, https://www.afr.com/policy/foreign-affairs/aukus-is-a-good-plan-b-for-china-but-let-s-not-bring-on-cold-war-2-0-20210920-p58ta8.

252 Gareth Evans, 'Australian Must Hold US to "No Quid Pro Quo" Guarantee with AUKUS', *The Australian Financial Review*, 23 September 2021, https://www.afr.com/policy/foreign-affairs/australia-must-hold-us-to-no-quid-pro-quo-guarantee-with-aukus-20210923-p58u3m.

253 Morrison, Press Conference, 16 September 2021.

254 The best sources for Morrison's foreign policy thinking up to September 2021 were his 9 June 2021 USAsia Centre Perth Address, 'A World Order that Favours Freedom', https://www.pm.gov.au/media/address-perth-usasia-centre-perth-wa; his 23 November 2020 UK Policy Exchange Virtual Address, https://www.pm.gov.au/media/uk-policy-exchange-virtual-address; his 1 July 2020 Defence Strategic Update Address, https://www.pm.gov.au/media/address-launch-2020-defence-strategic-update; and his April 2021 extended interview with the author, quoted throughout this Paper.

255 Morrison, interview with the author, April 2021.

256 Condoleezza Rice, '2002 Wriston Lecture: A Balance of Power that Favours Freedom', New York, 1 October 2002, https://www.manhattan-institute.org/html/2002-wriston-lecture-balance-power-favors-freedom-5566.html.

257 Morrison, interview with the author, April 2021.

258 Payne, interview with the author, October 2021.

259 Morrison, Address to the Perth USAsia Centre, 2021.

260 Ibid.

261 Maude, interview with the author, April 2021.

262 Morrison, Address to the Perth USAsia Centre, 2021

263 Ibid.

264 Gyngell, interview with the author, April 2021.

265 Marise Payne, Address to Australia China Business Council, 5 August 2021, https://www.foreignminister.gov.au/minister/marise-payne/speech/address-australia-china-business-council.

266 Adamson, National Press Club Address, 2021.

267 Jakobson, interview with the author, October 2021.

268 Varghese, interview with the author, April 2021.

269 Miller, interview with the author, April 2021.

270 Varghese, interview with the author, April 2021.

271 Adamson, ANU National Security College 10th Anniversary Lecture Series, 2020.

272 Morrison, interview with the author, April 2021.

273 Peter Dutton, Interview with David Speers, ABC, Insiders, 30 April 2021, https://www.minister.defence.gov.au/ minister/peter-dutton/transcripts/interview-david-speers-abc-insiders.

274 Payne, interview with the author, October 2021.

275 Maude, interview with the author, April 2021; and Richard Maude, 'China Redux: Business and the Contest for Power in the Indo-Pacific', Speech to the New Zealand China Business Summit, 3 May 2021, https://asiasociety. org/australia/china-redux-business-and-contest-power-indo-pacific.

276 Richardson, interview with the author, October 2021.

Lowy Institute
Penguin Specials

PENGUIN
SPECIALS

RECONSTRUCTION

John Edwards

A LOWY INSTITUTE PAPER

What kind of future do Australians have?

Until the coronavirus pandemic, nearly two-thirds of Australians had never experienced an economic slump in their working lives. Indeed, nearly half were not yet born when the Australian economy last tipped into recession. Creating a path for Australia through these difficult times requires a careful assessment of where we have come from, where we are, and where we are going.

This Paper, by one of Australia's leading economic voices, examines the fractured state of the global economy and financial system, the ailing US economy and its epic contest with China, the global economic order, and what it all means for us.

RECONSTRUCTION

John Edwards

PENGUIN
SPECIALS

MAN OF CONTRADICTIONS

Ben Bland

A LOWY INSTITUTE PAPER

From a riverside shack to the presidential palace, Joko Widodo surged to the top of Indonesian politics on a wave of hope for change. However, six years into his presidency, the former furniture maker is struggling to deliver the reforms that Indonesia desperately needs. Despite promising to build Indonesia into an Asian powerhouse, Jokowi, as he is known, has faltered in the face of crises, from COVID-19 to an Islamist mass movement.

Man of Contradictions, the first English-language biography of Jokowi, argues that the president embodies the fundamental contradictions of modern Indonesia. He is caught between democracy and authoritarianism, openness and protectionism, Islam and pluralism. Jokowi's incredible story shows what is possible in Indonesia – and it also shows the limits.

PENGUIN
SPECIALS

OUR VERY OWN BREXIT

Sam Roggeveen

A LOWY INSTITUTE PAPER

Could Australia have a Brexit moment?

There is a rarely spoken truth at the heart of Australian politics: it is dominated by two parties that voters no longer care about.

Around the democratic West, the public is drifting away from major parties, and politics is becoming hollow. In Europe, populists have been the beneficiaries. In Britain, the result was Brexit.

Australian politics is hollow, too. One of our declining parties could, in desperation, exploit an issue that ties Australia to Asia and which will determine our future security: immigration.